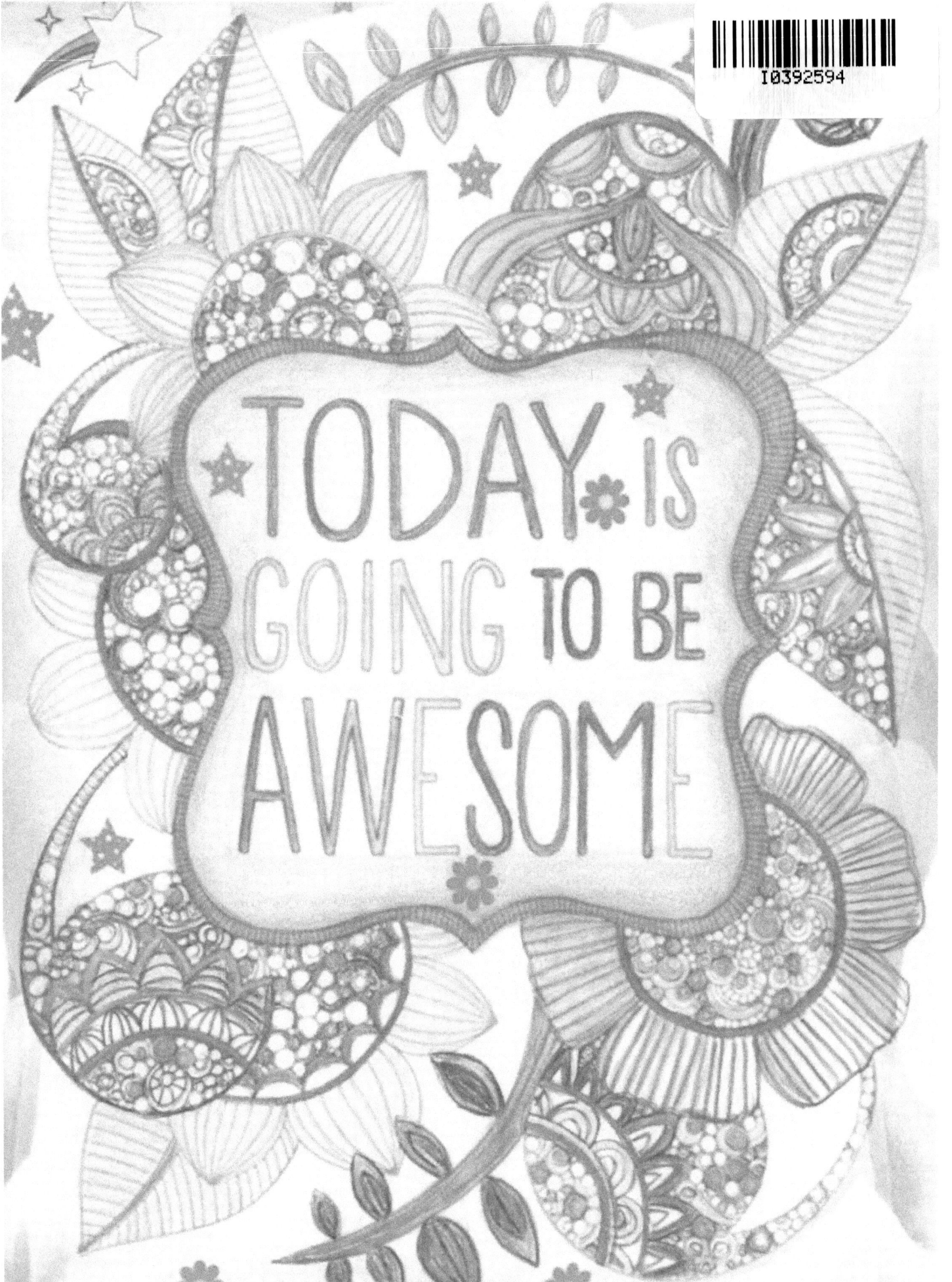

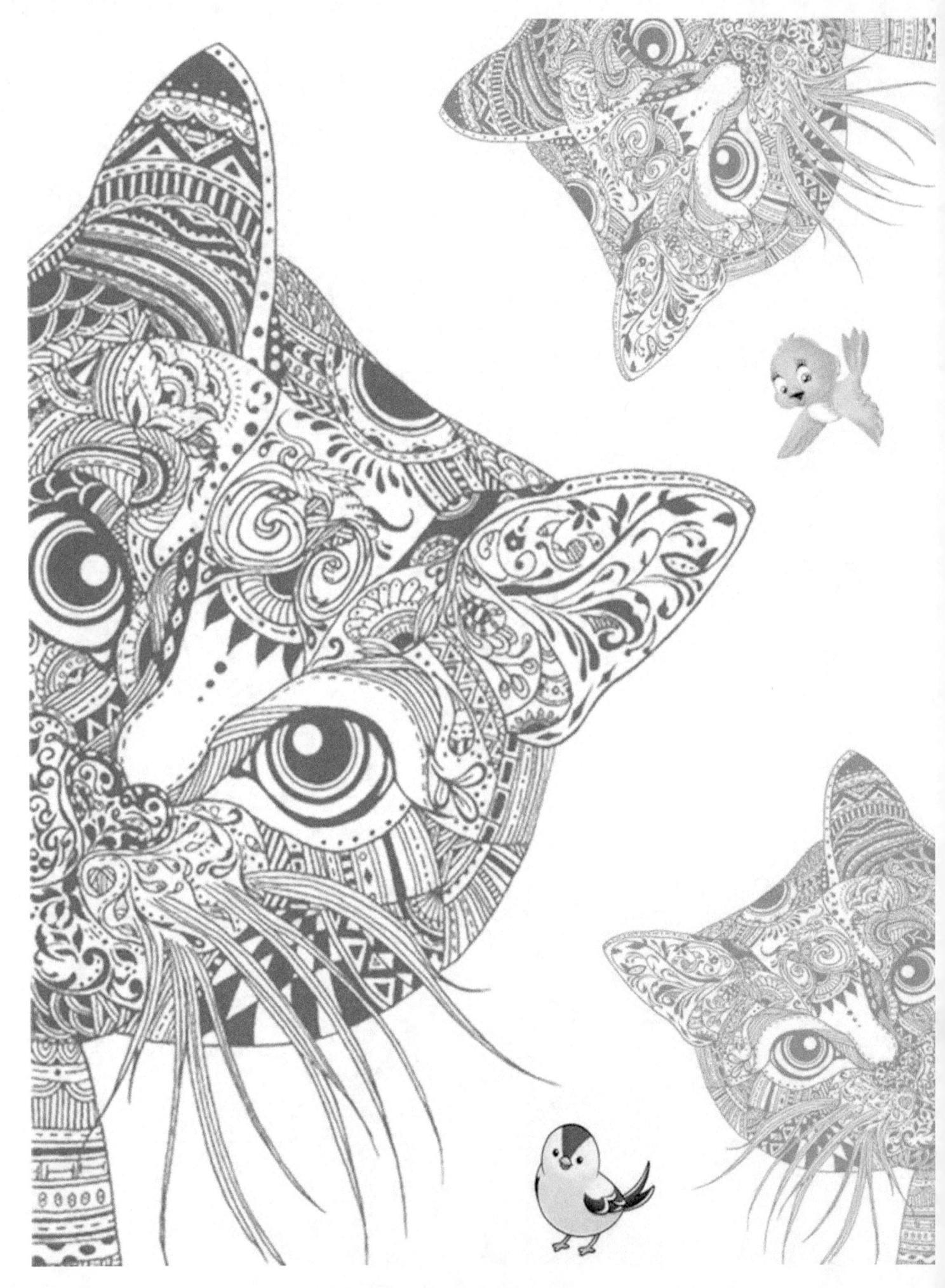

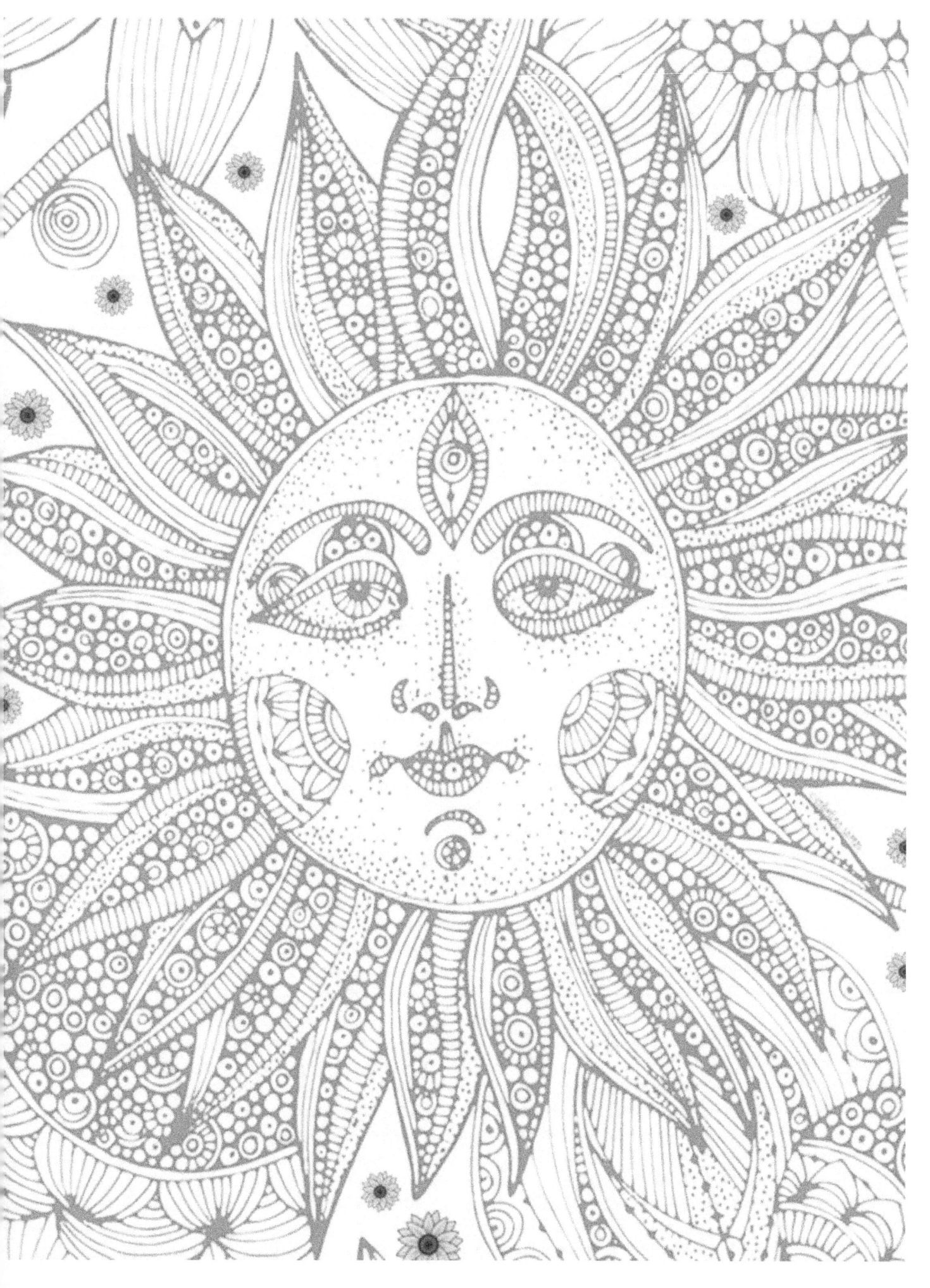

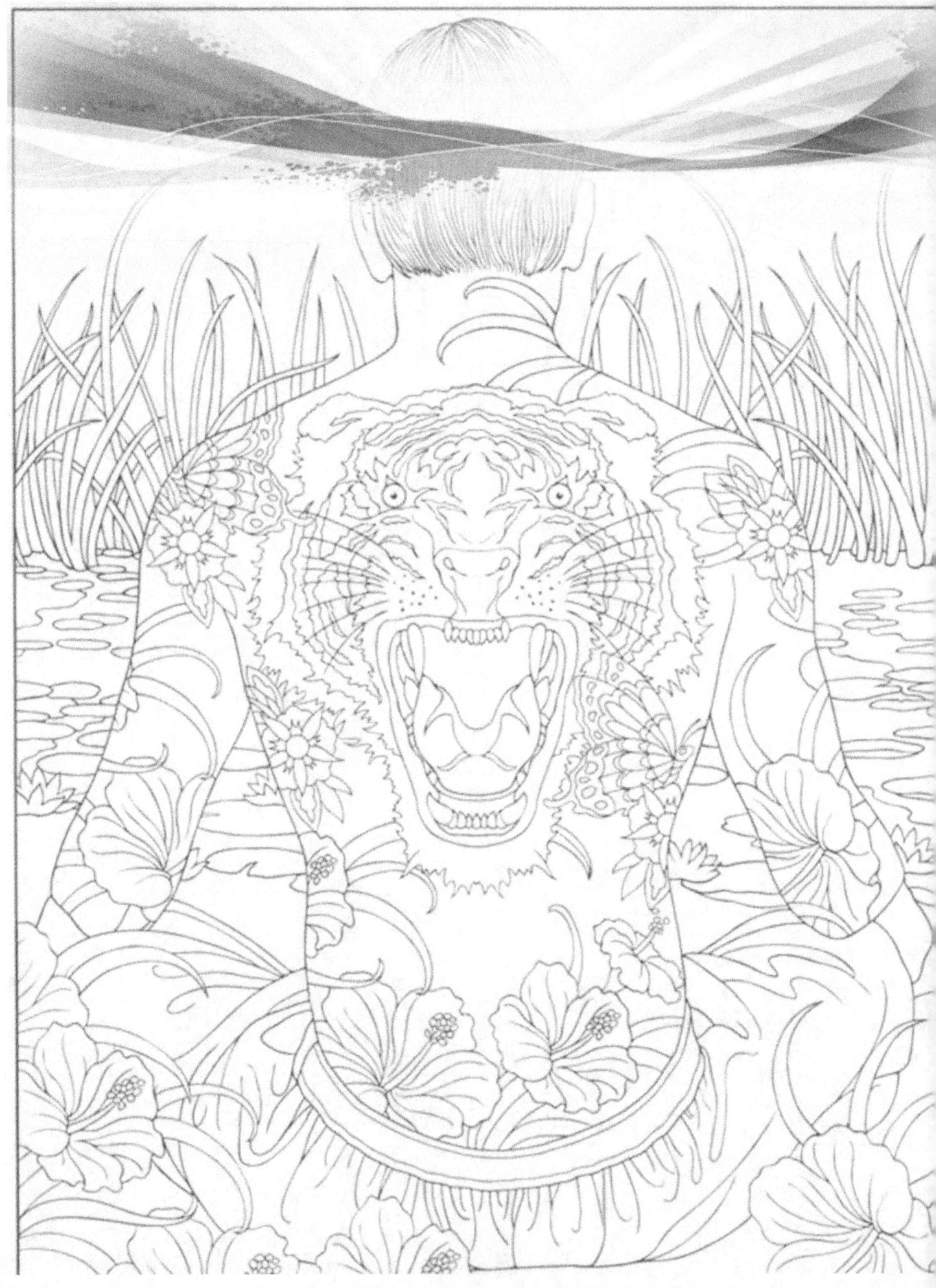

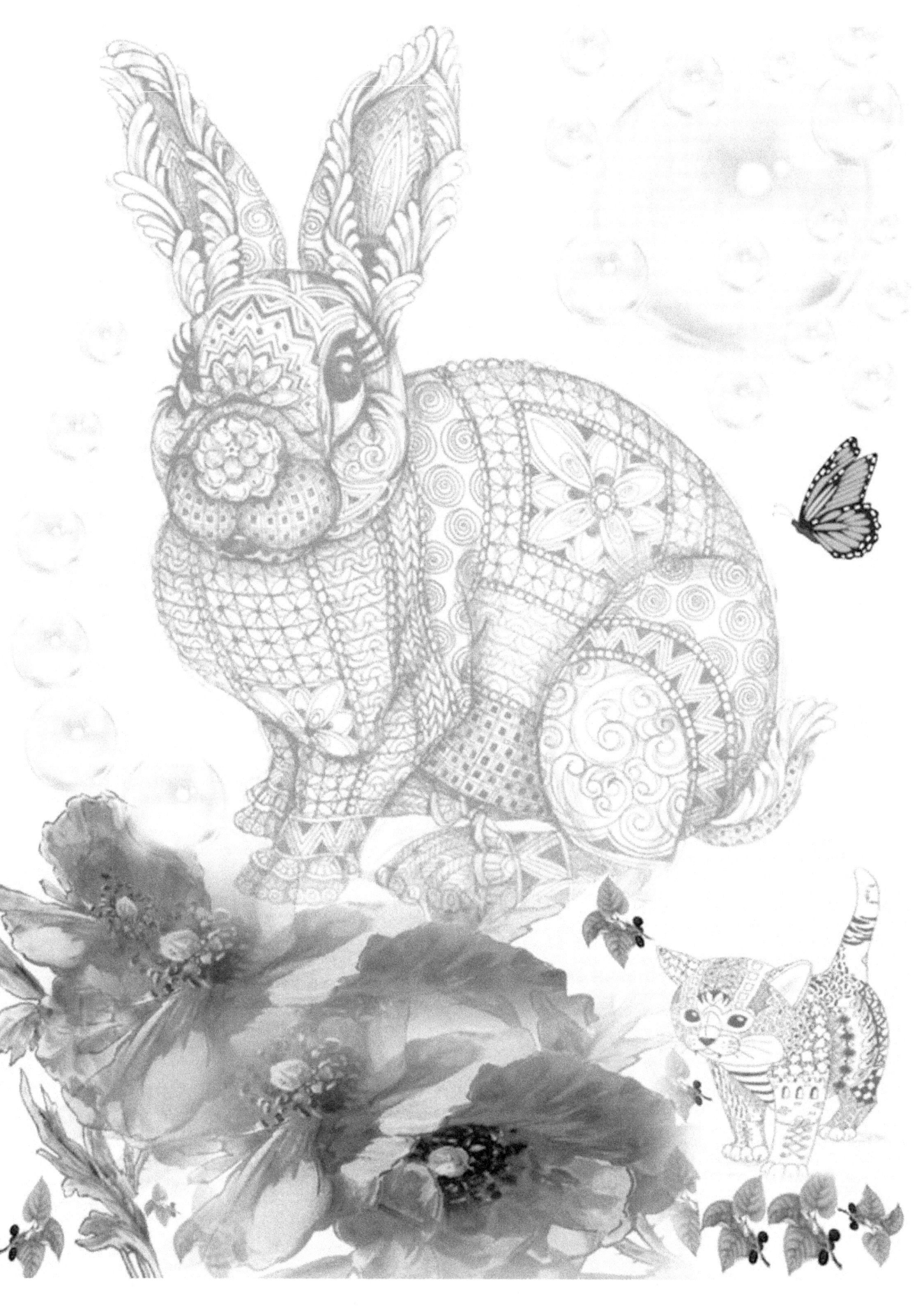

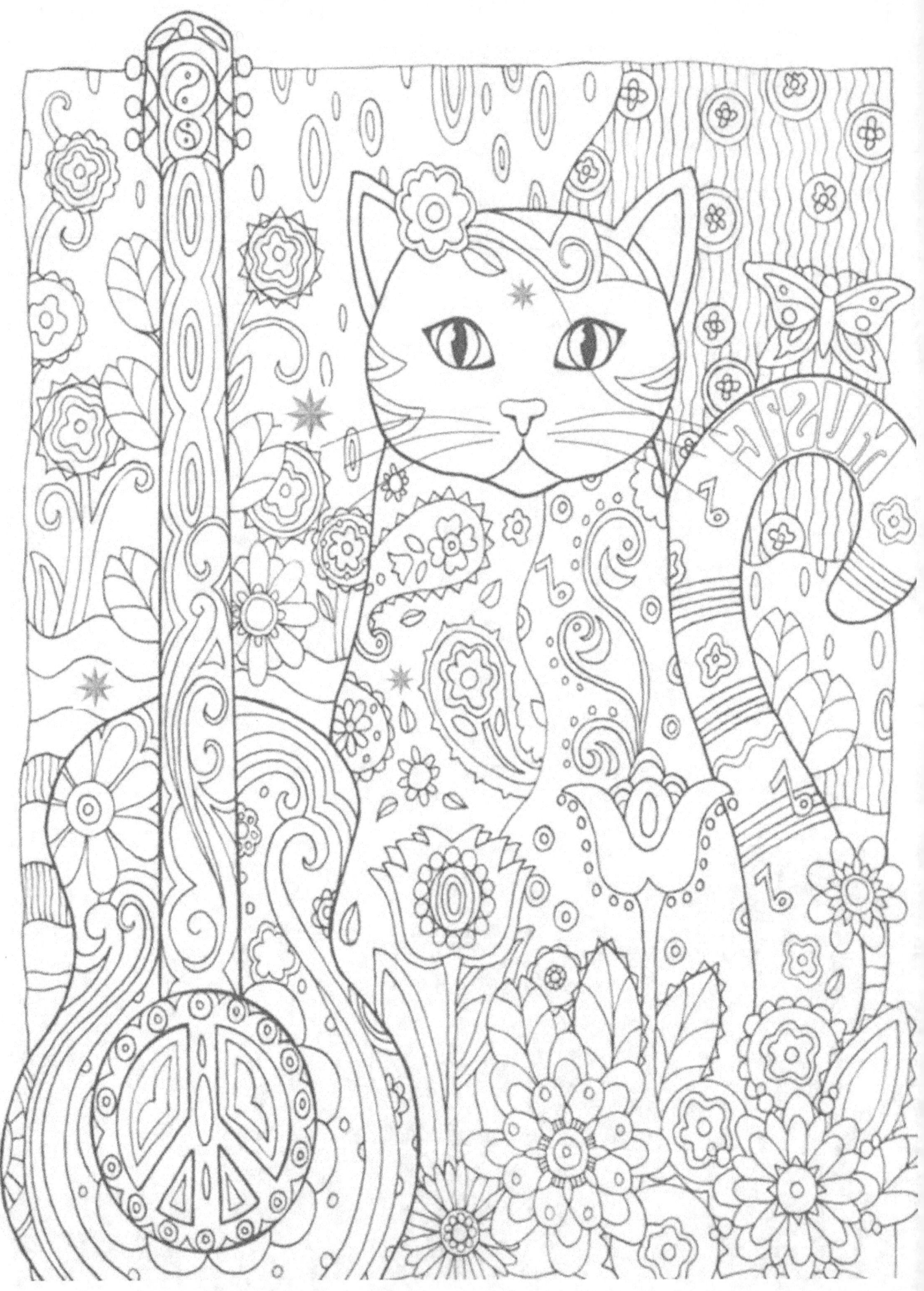

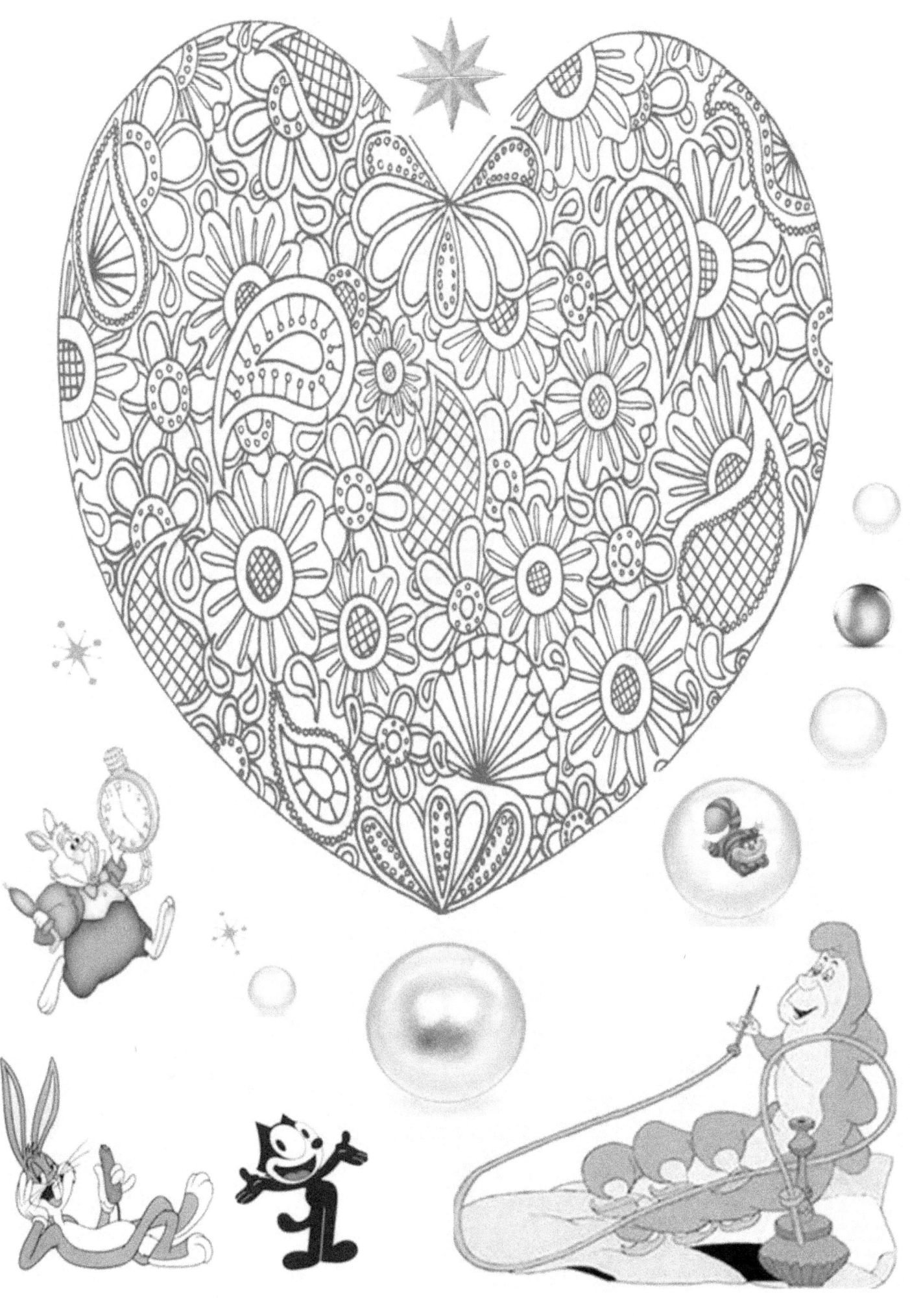

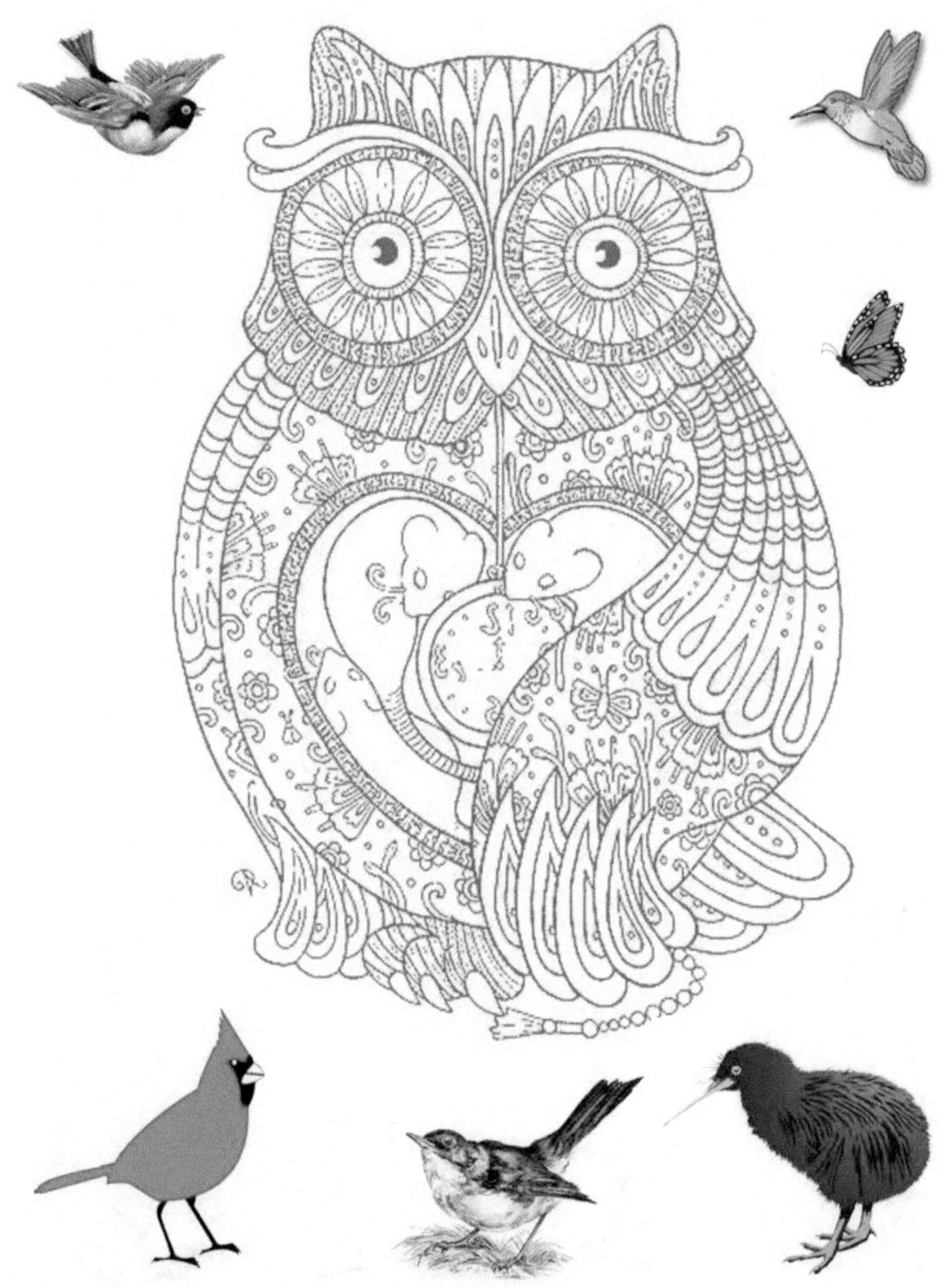

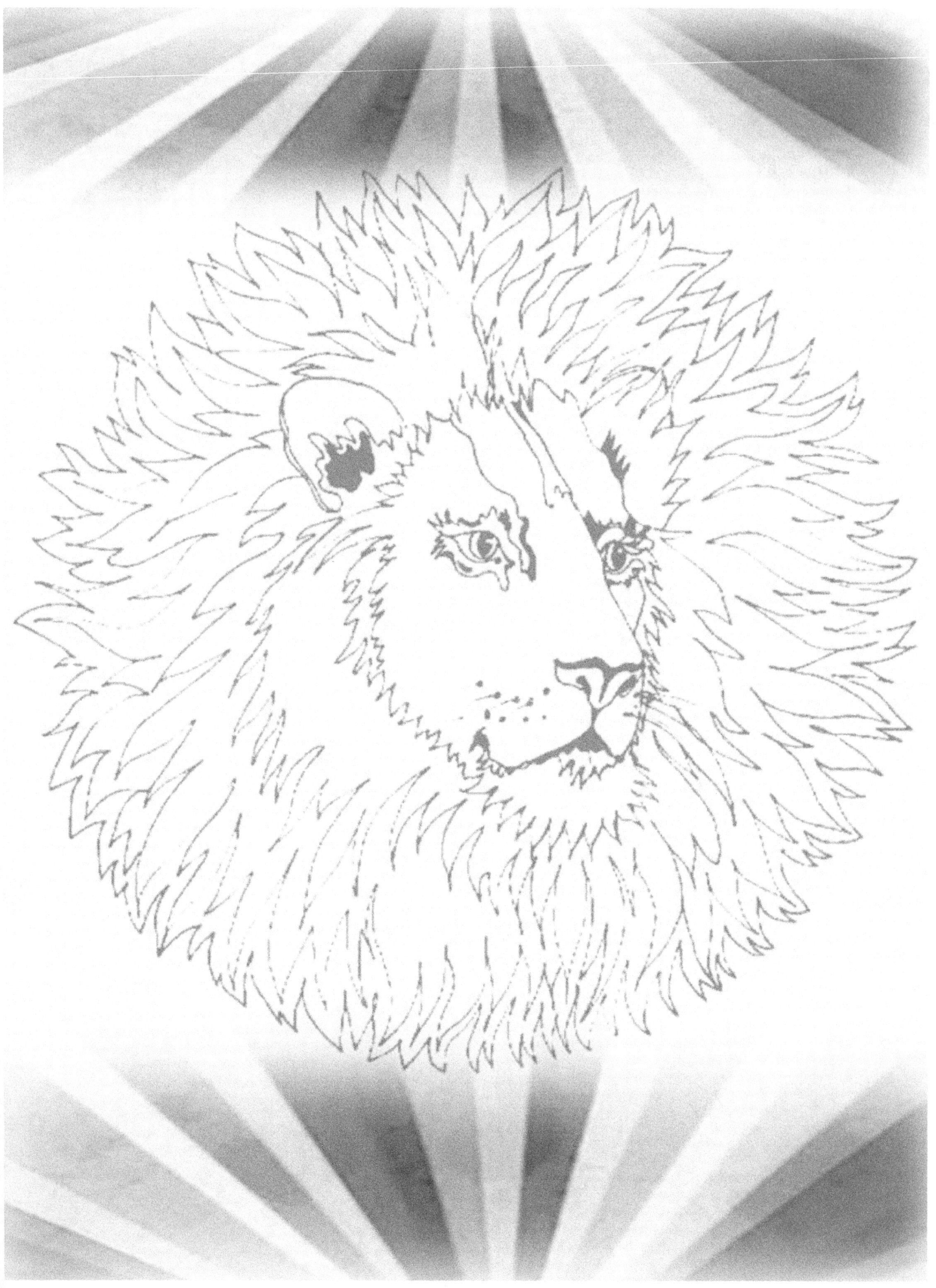

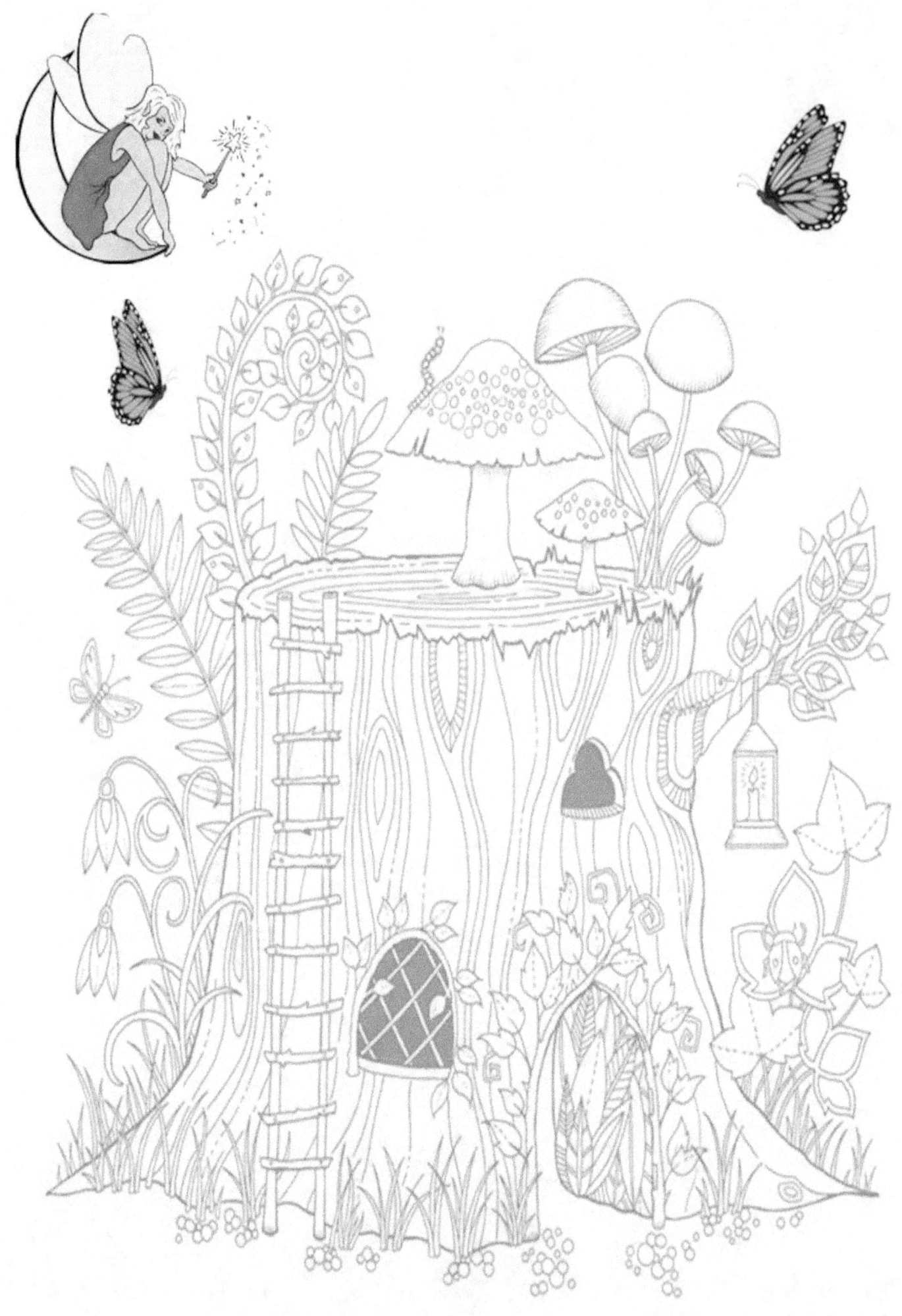

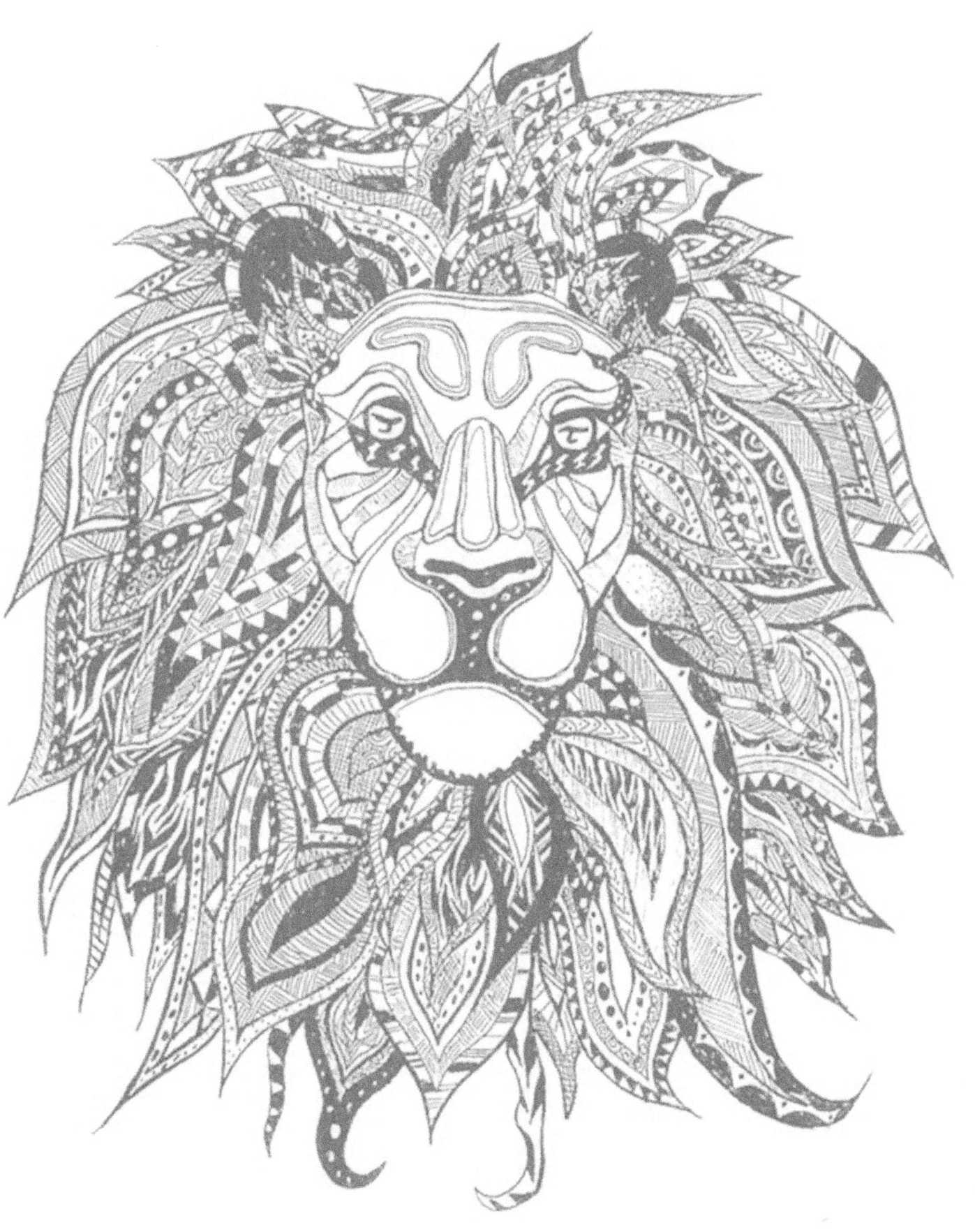

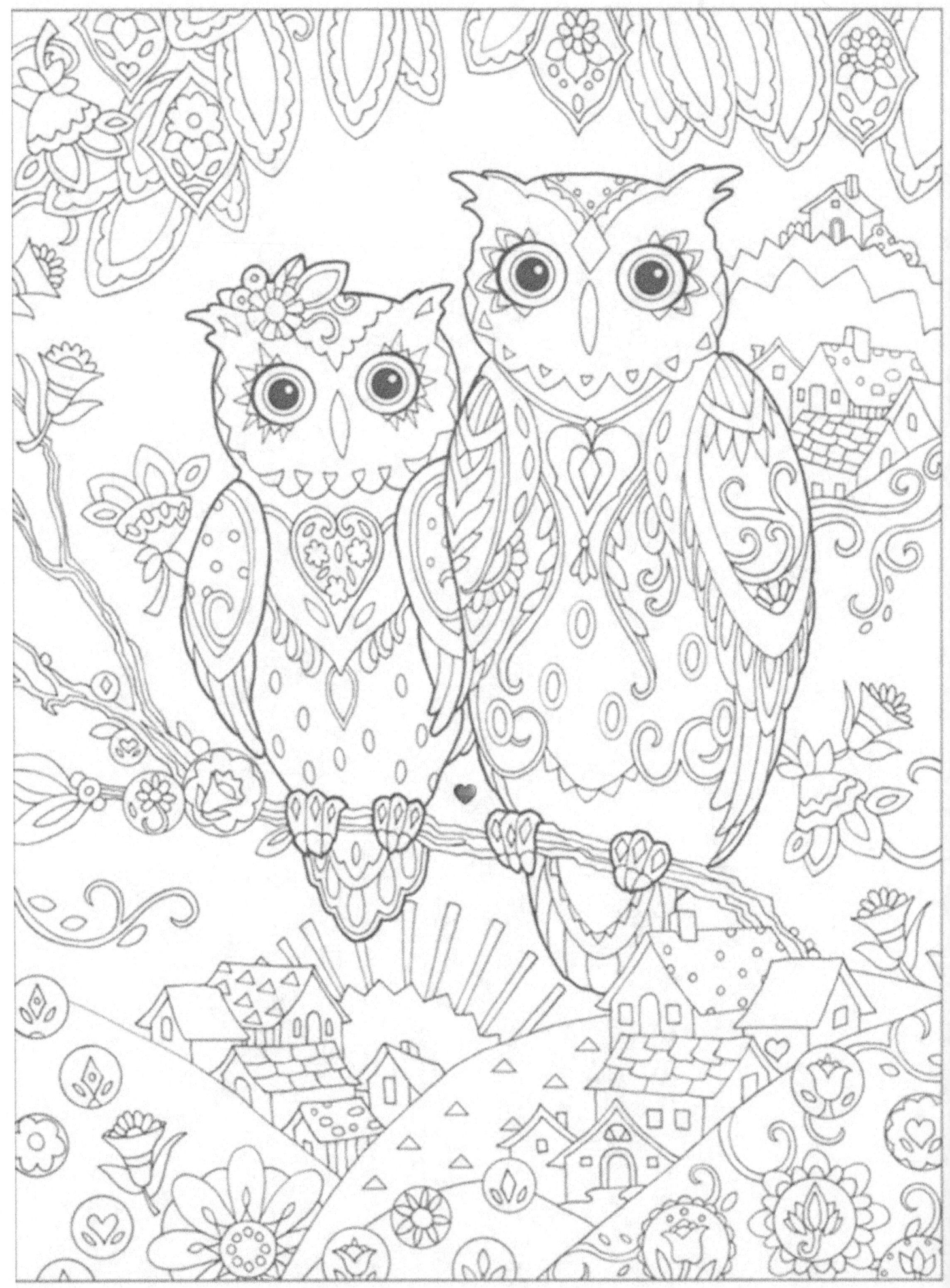

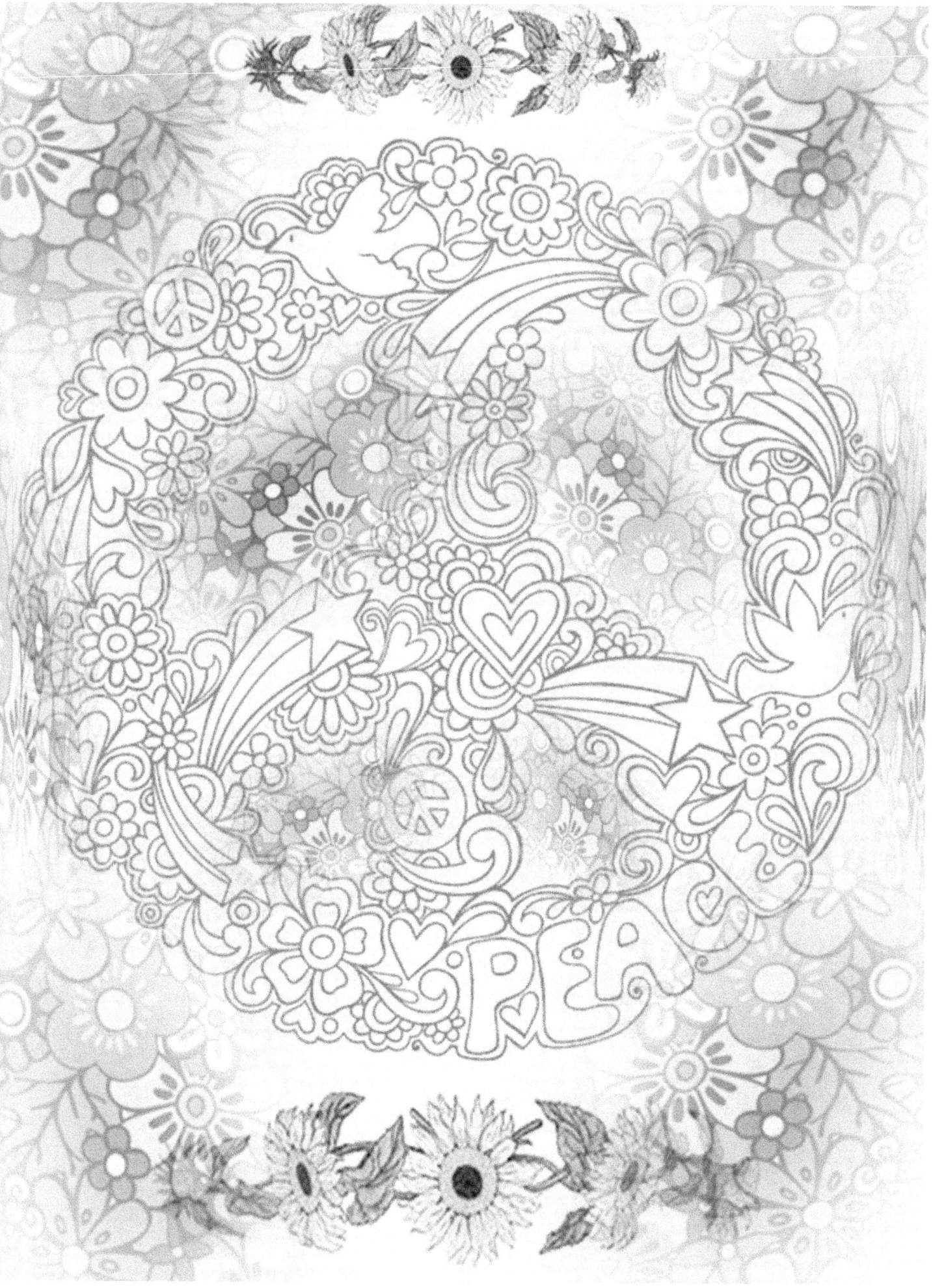

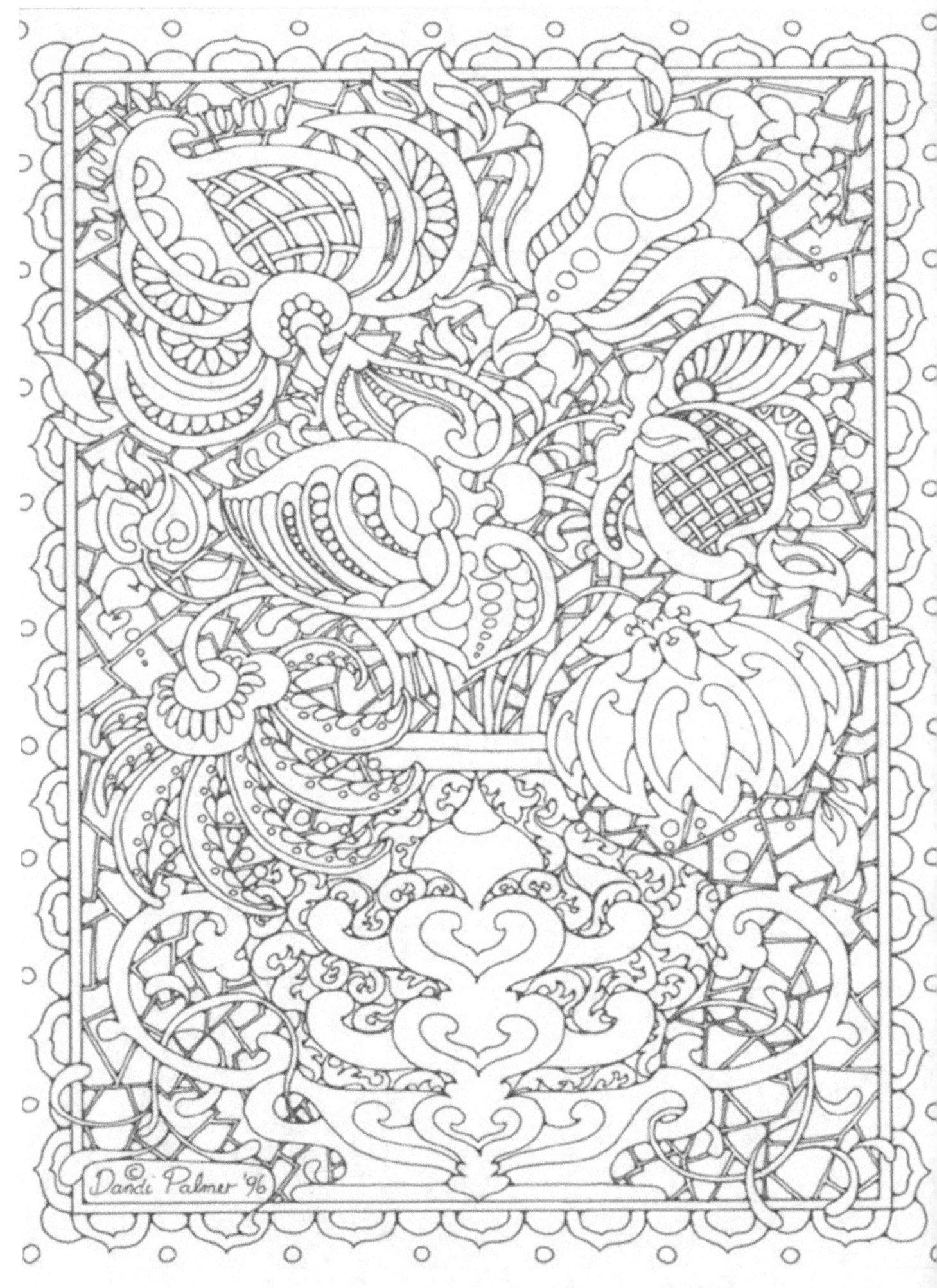

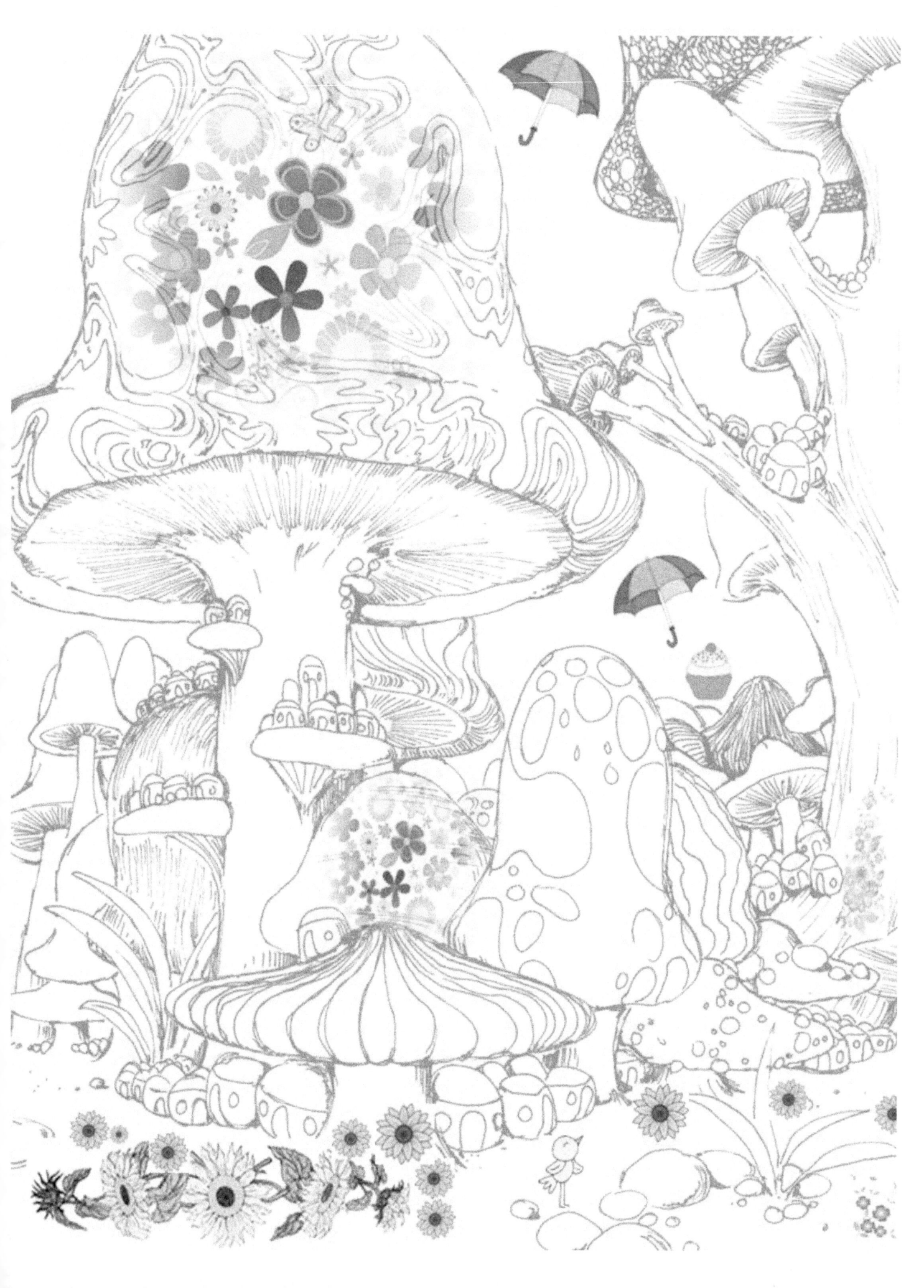

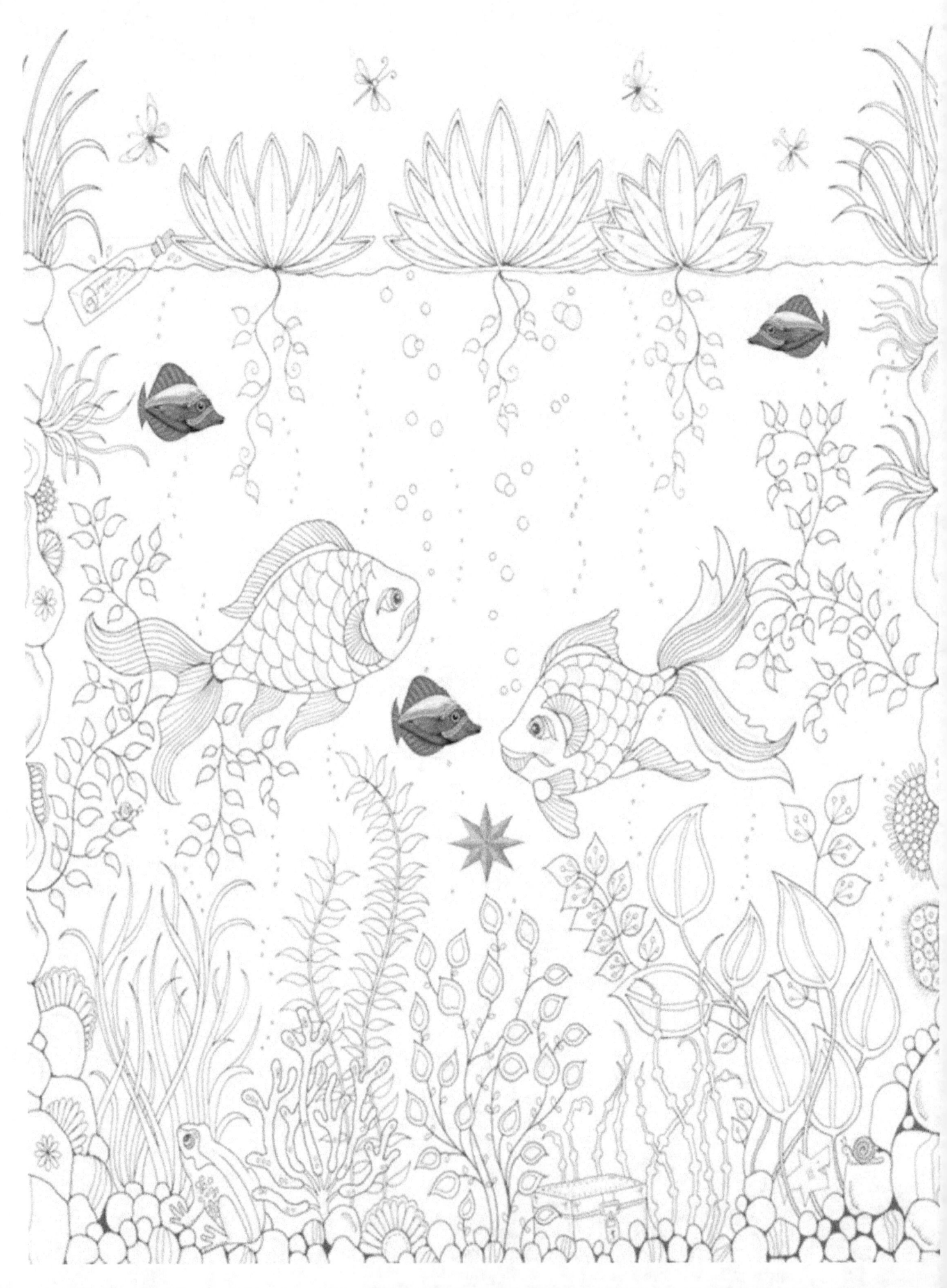

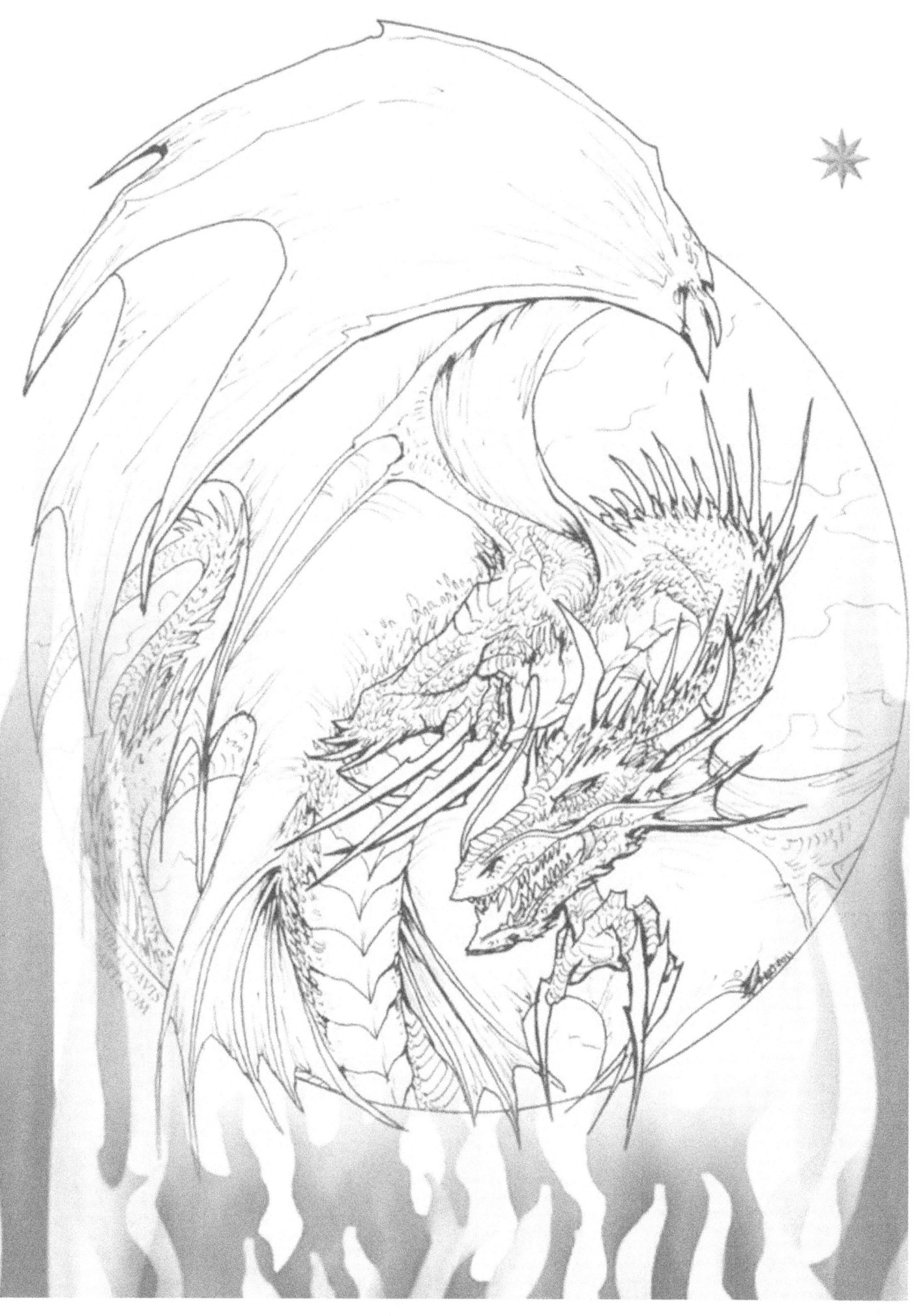

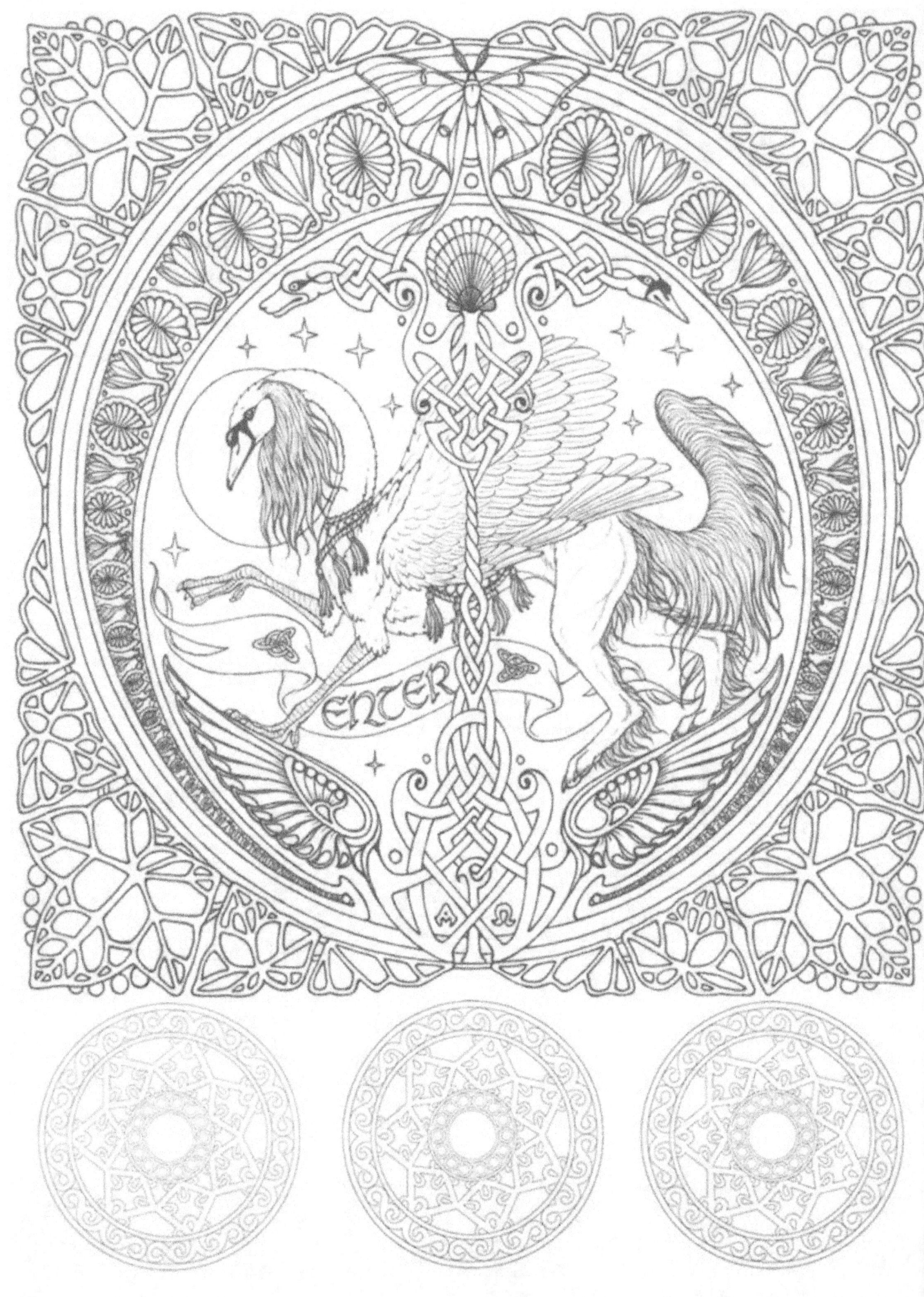

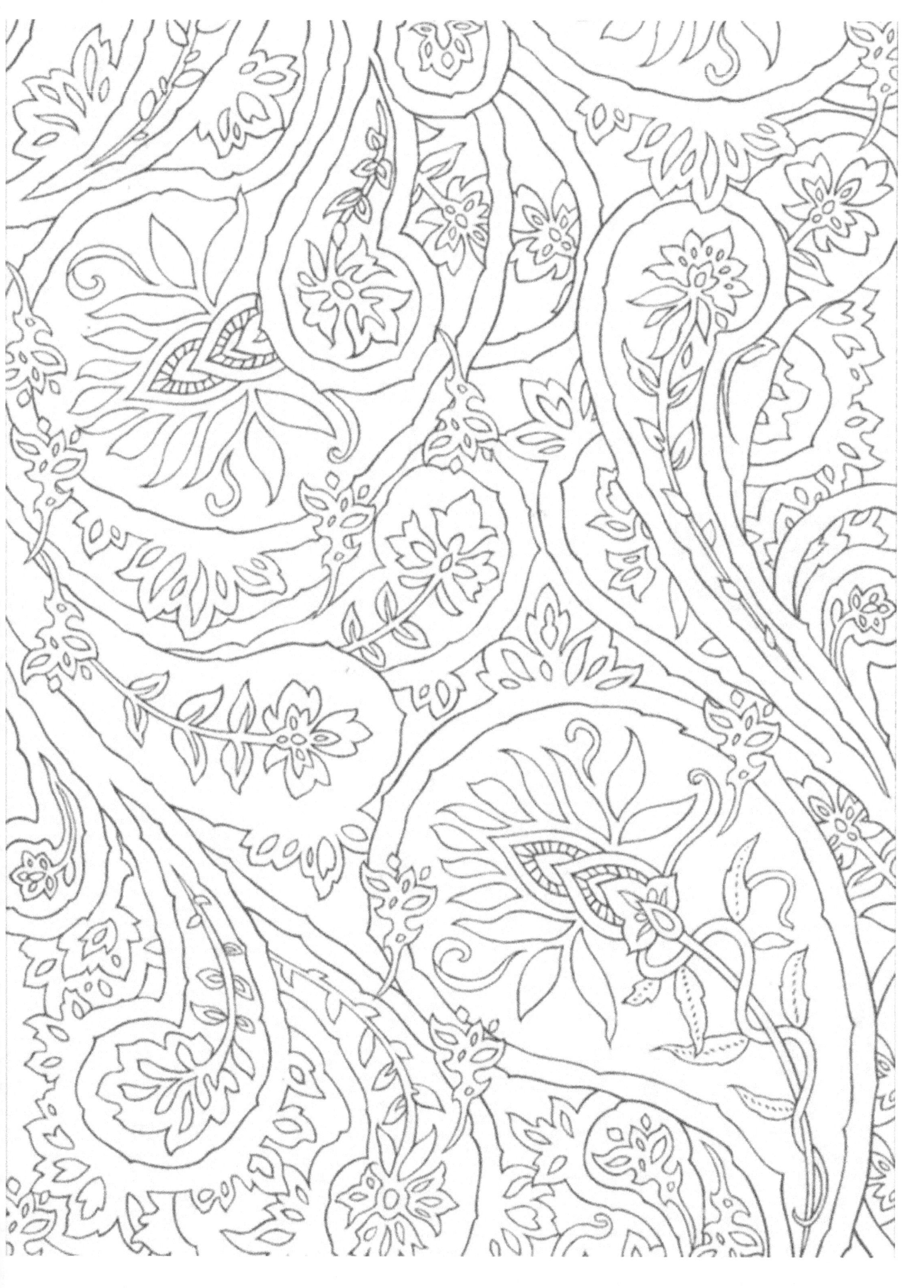

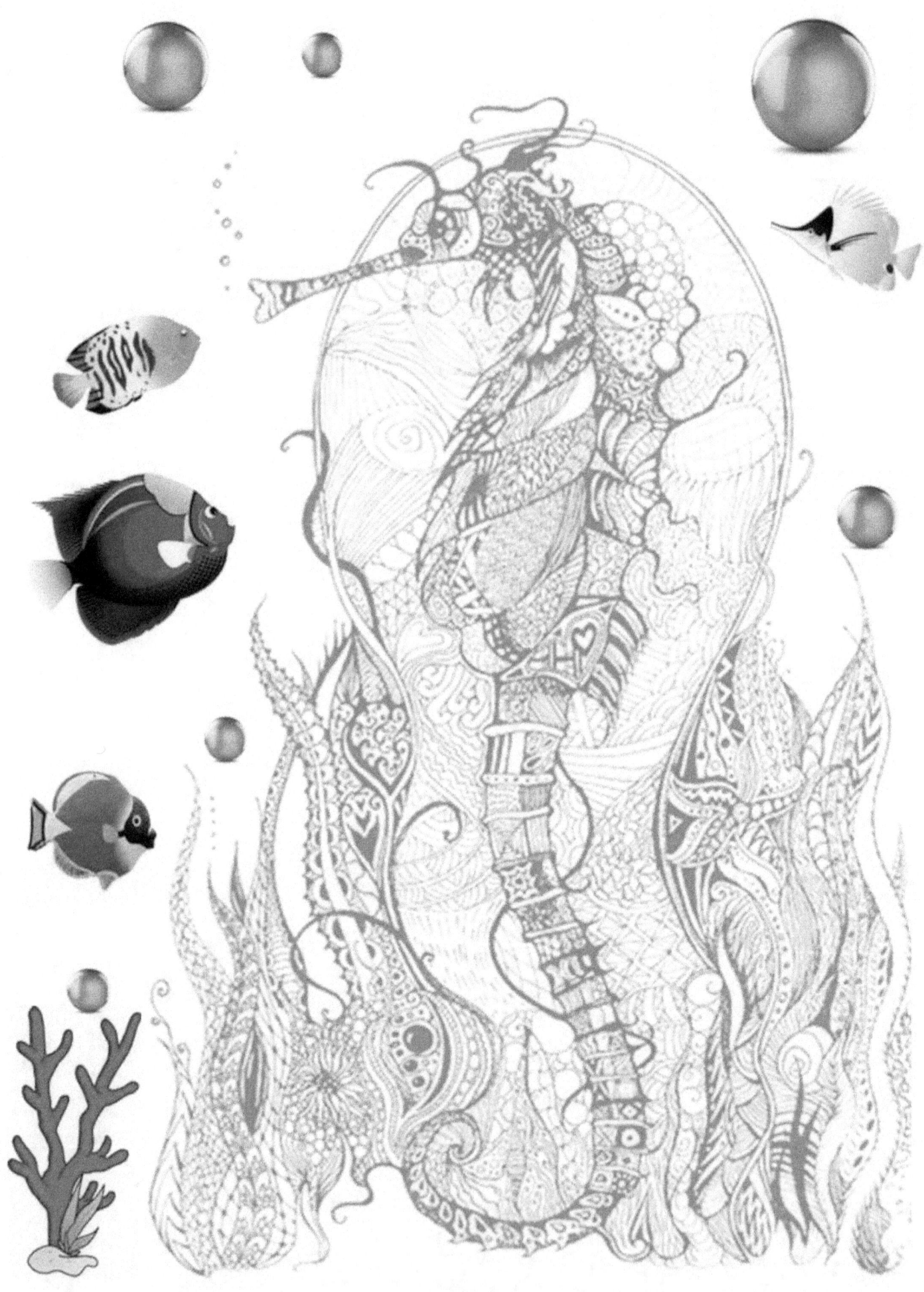

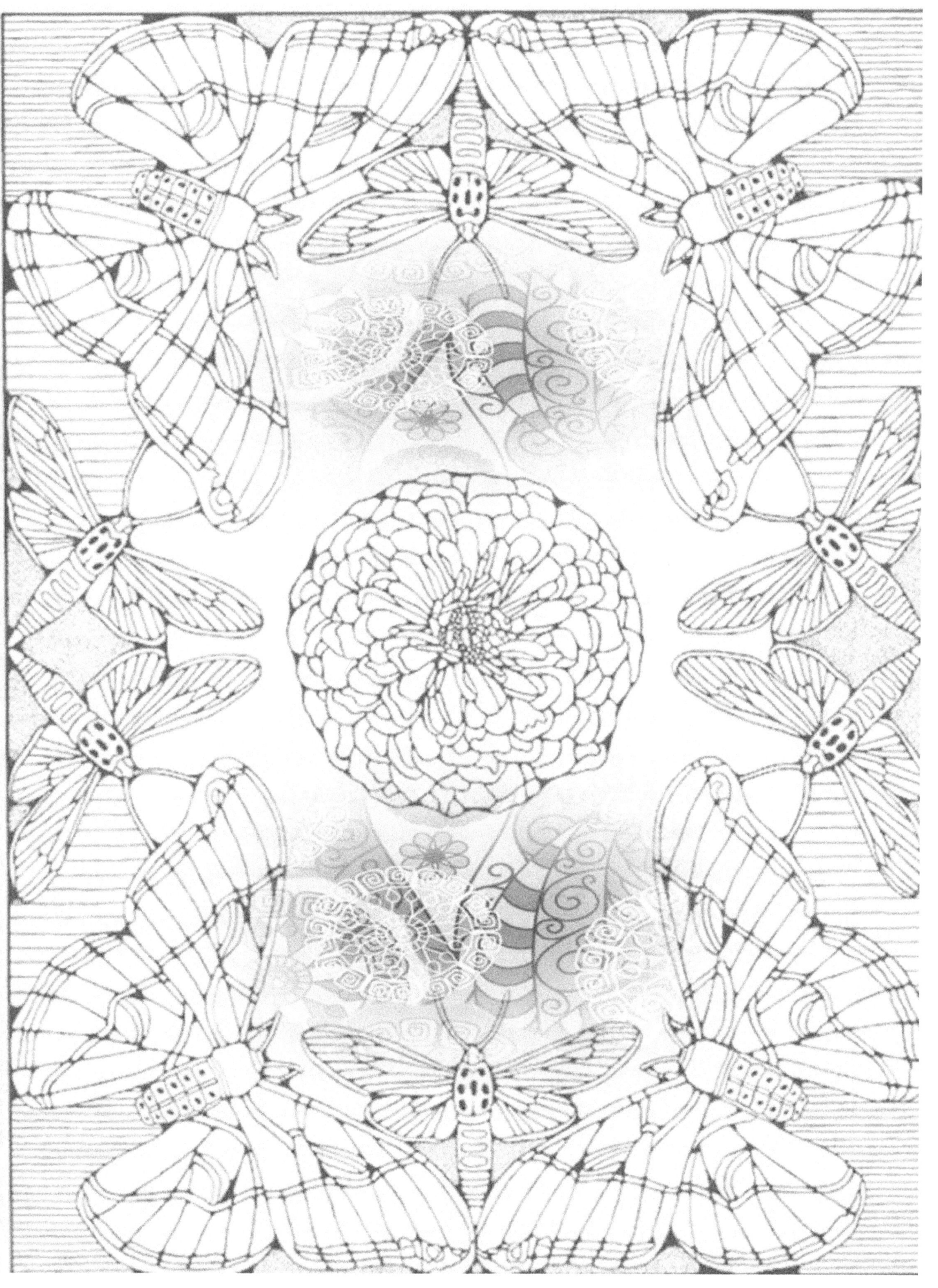

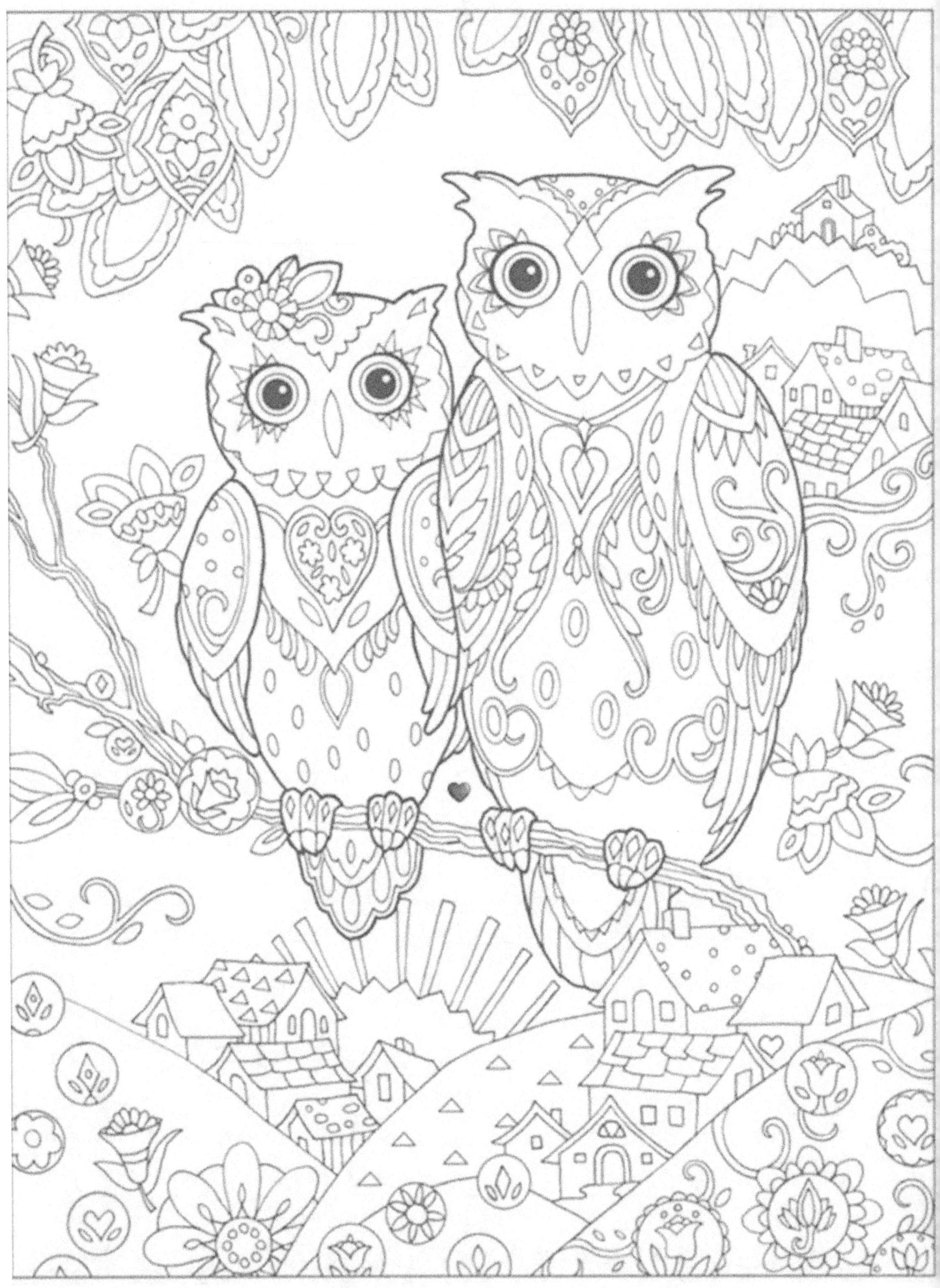

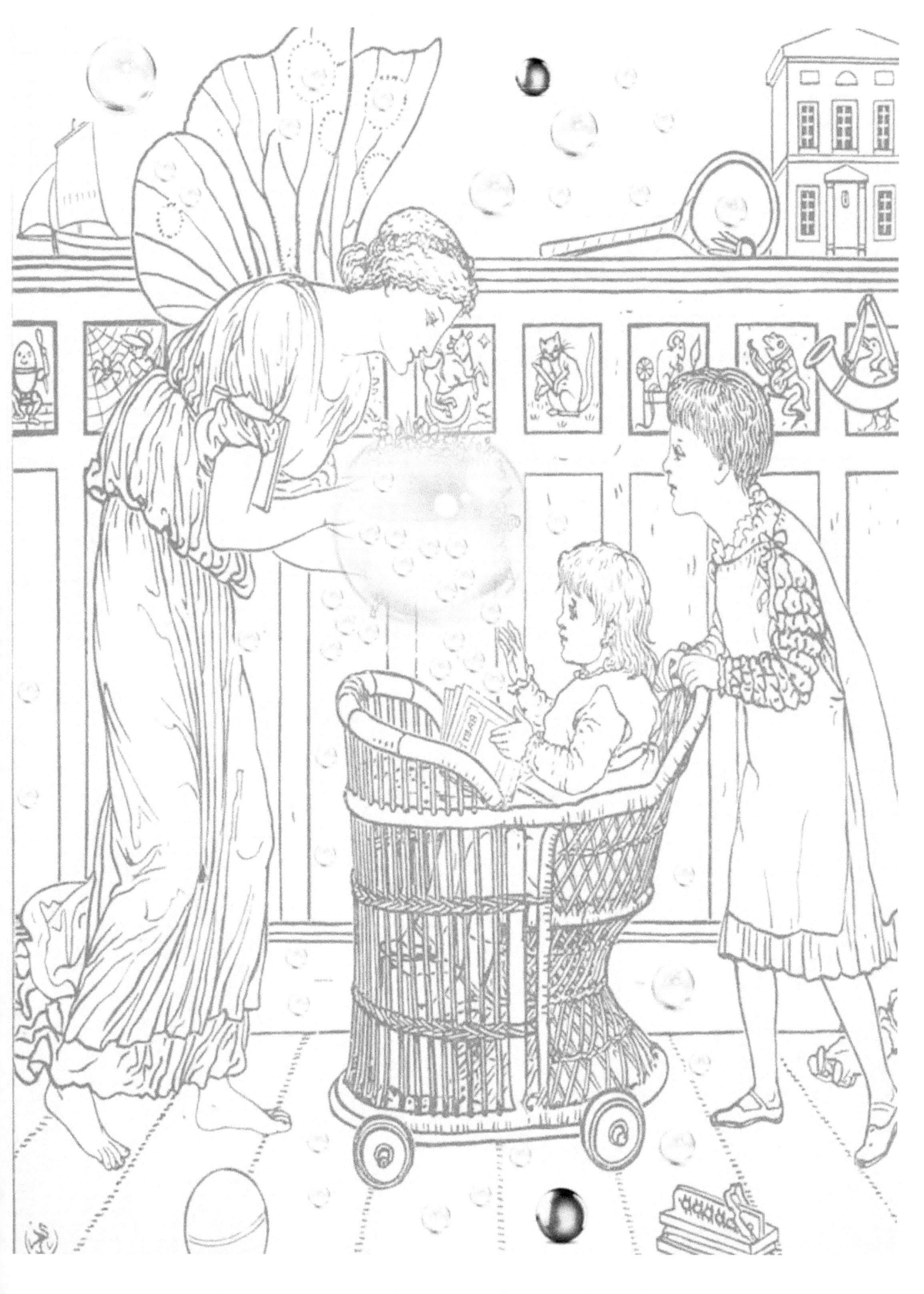

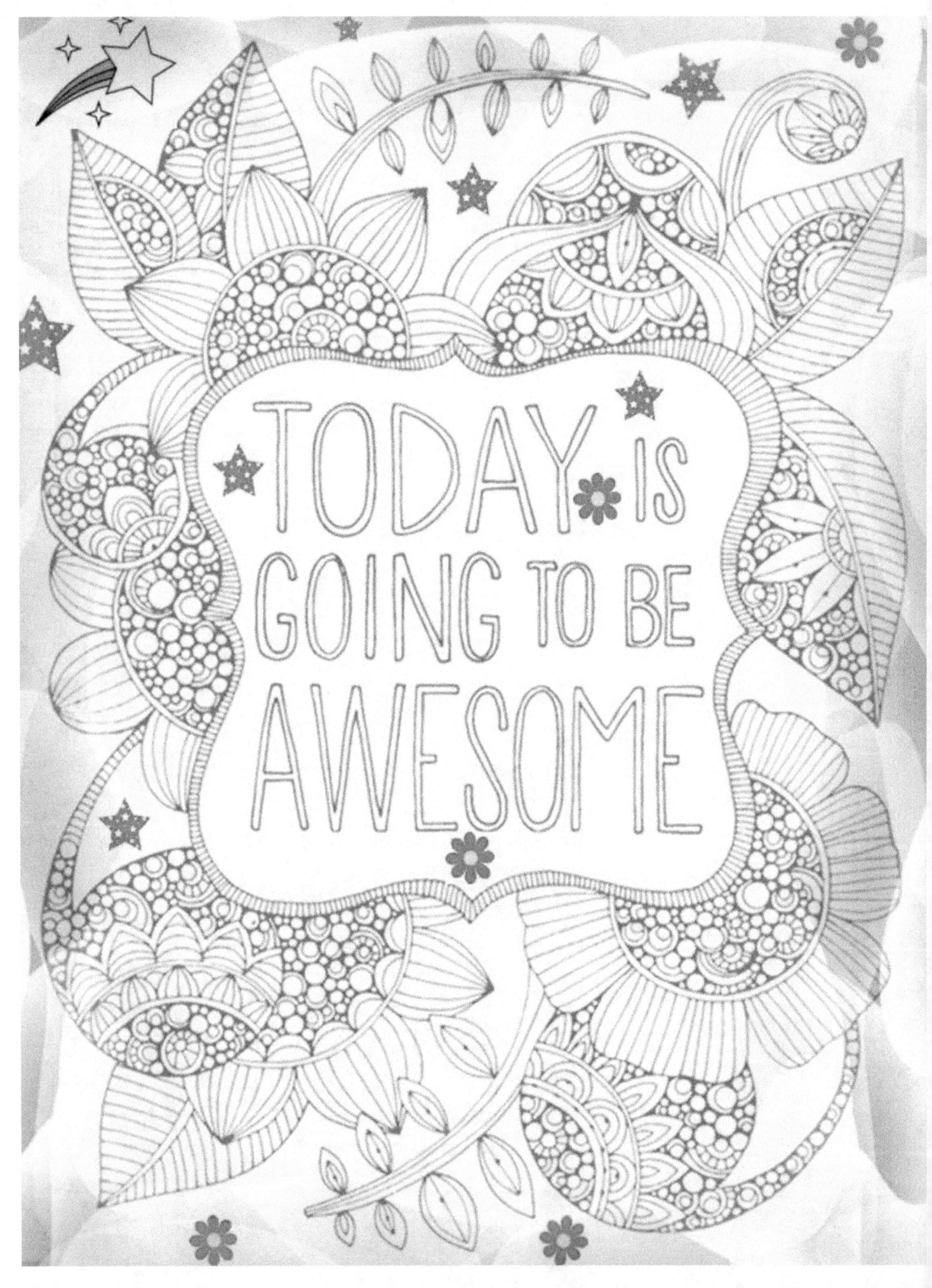

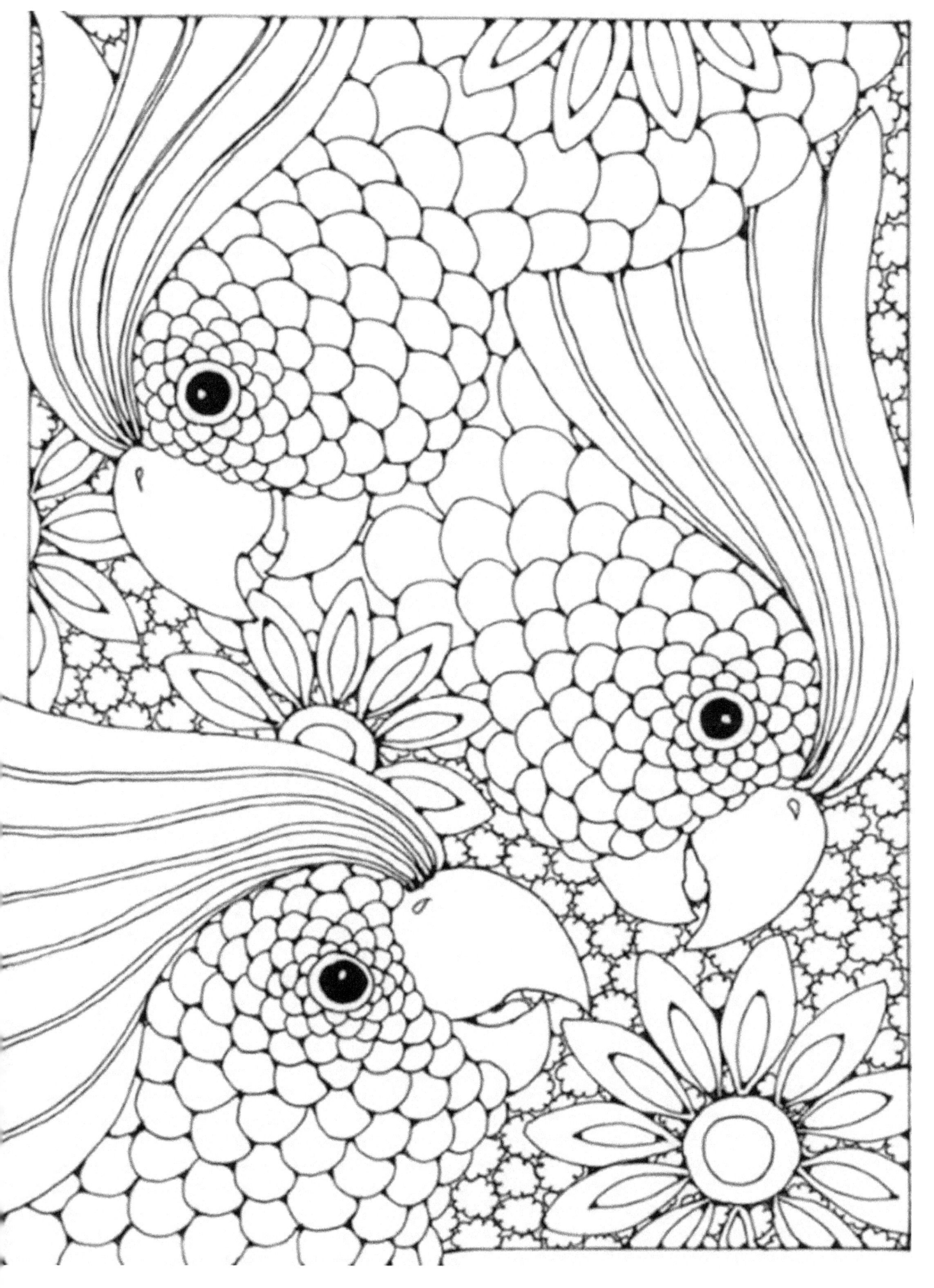

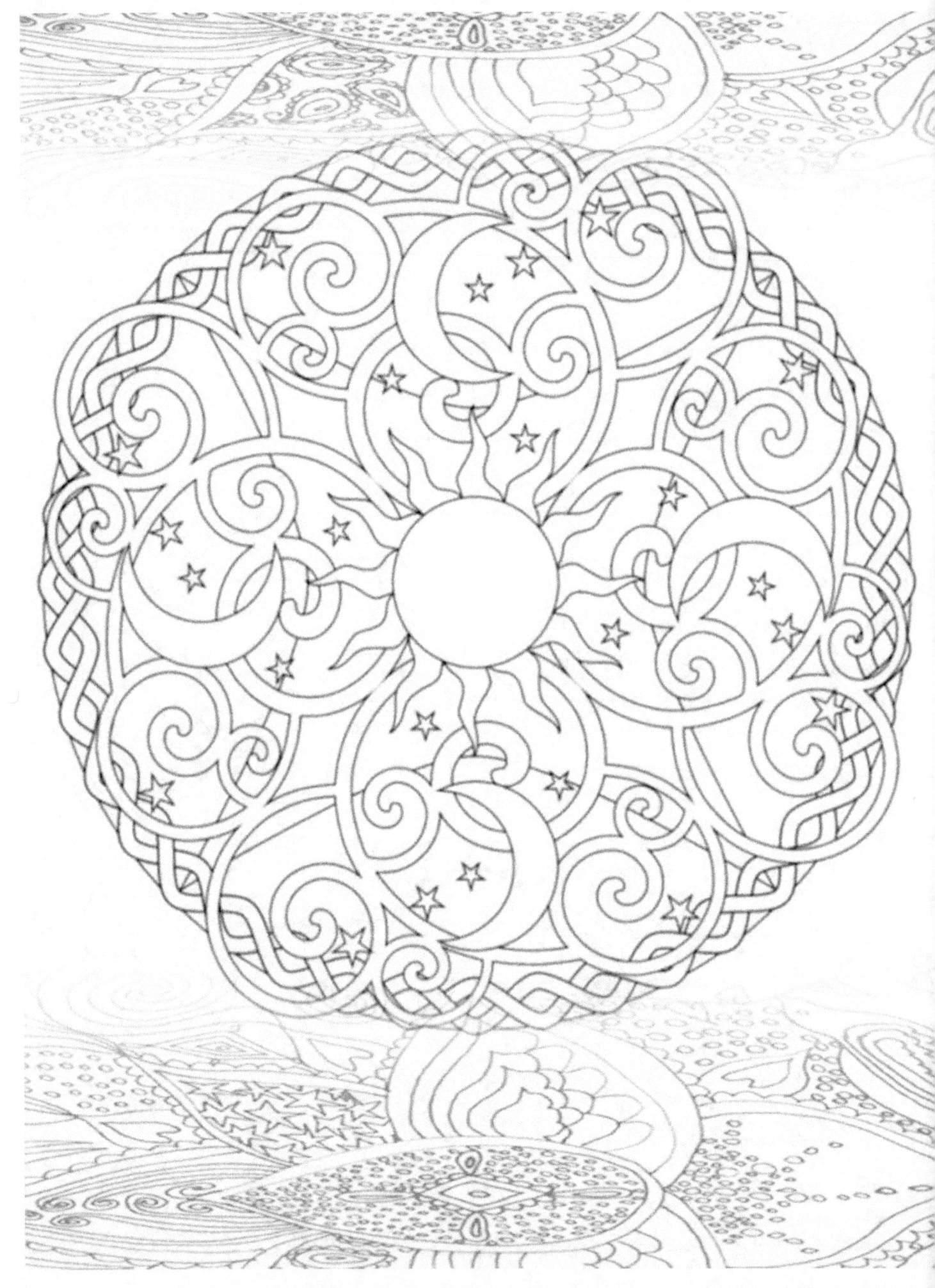

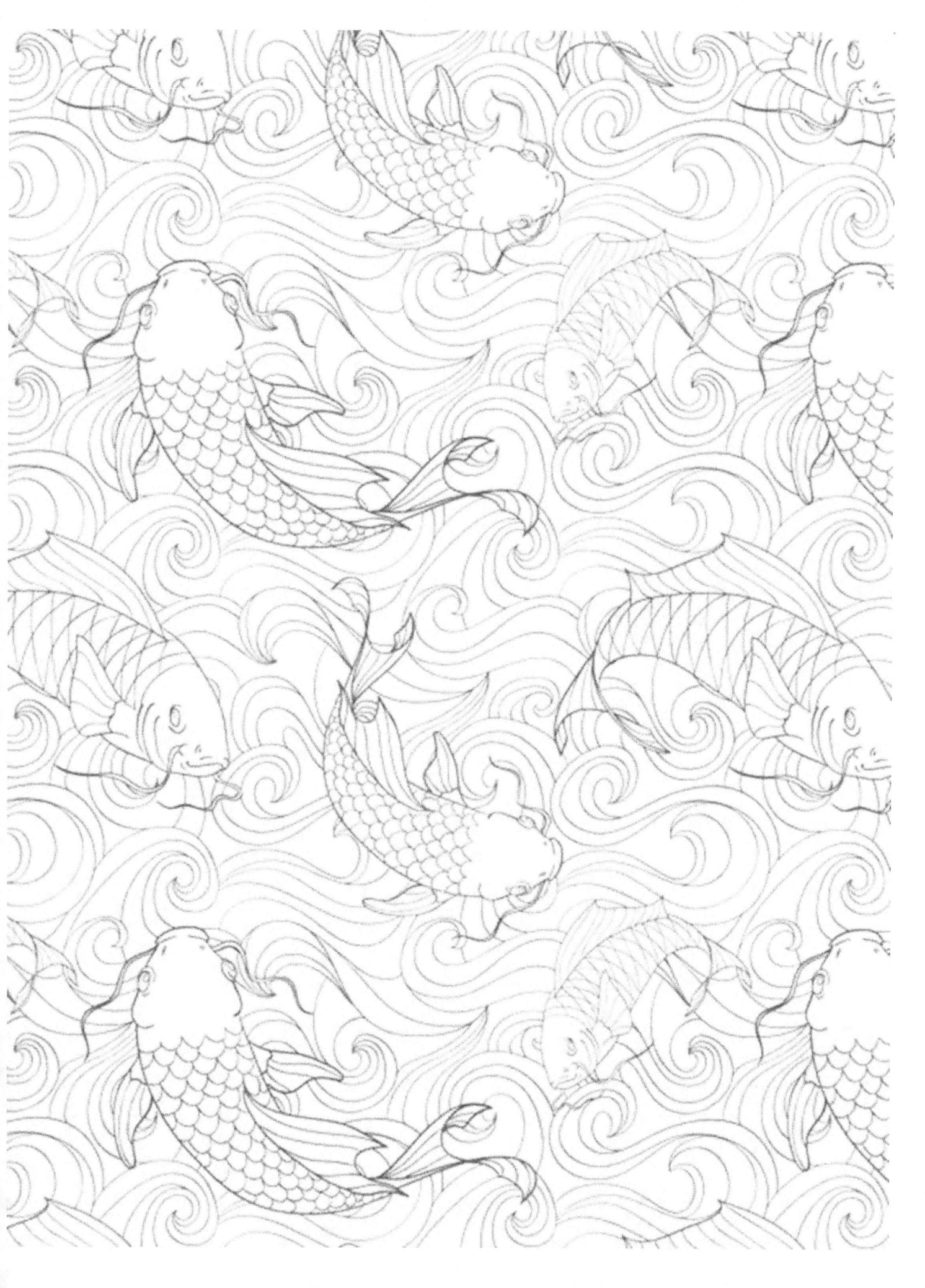

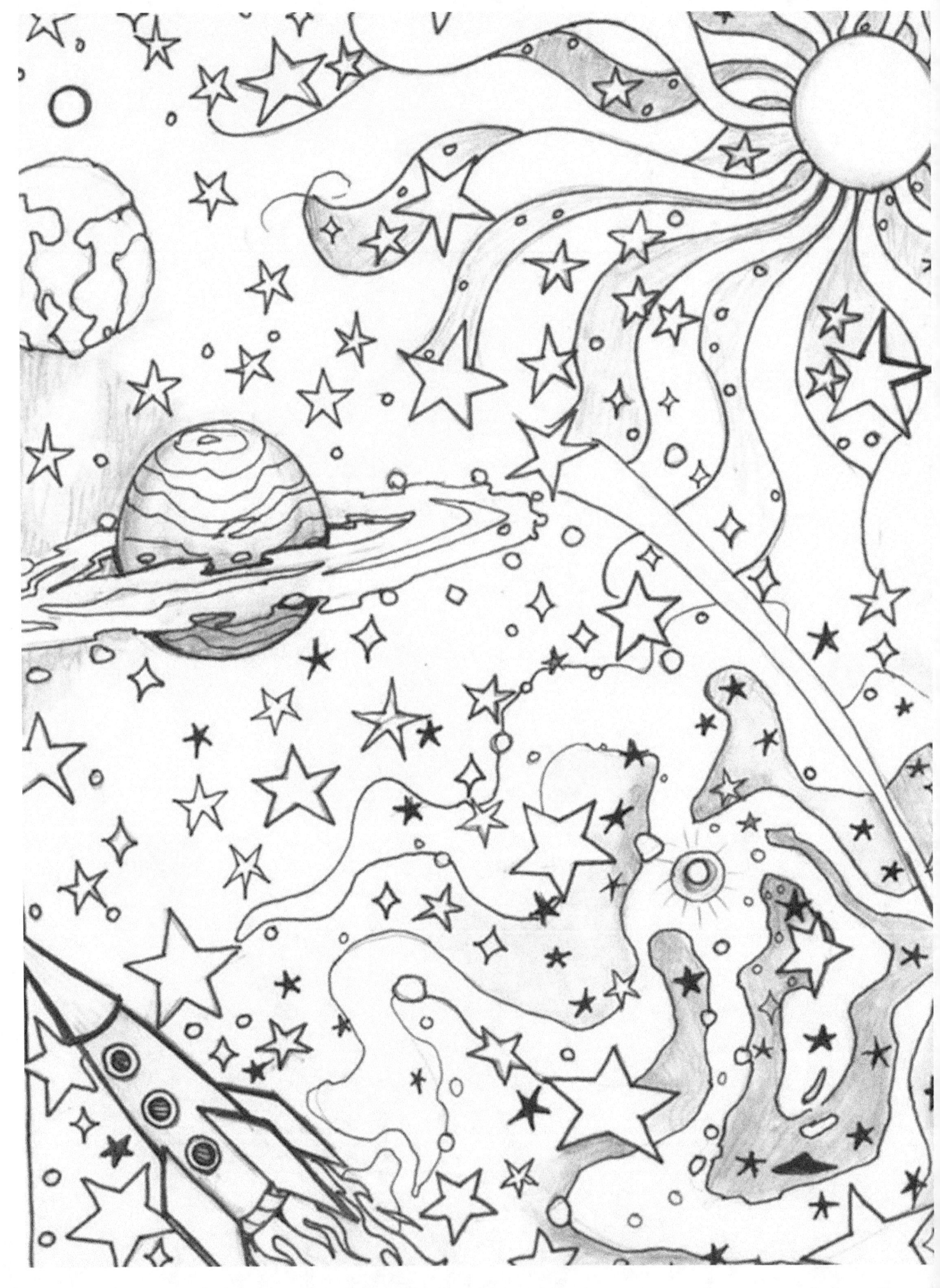

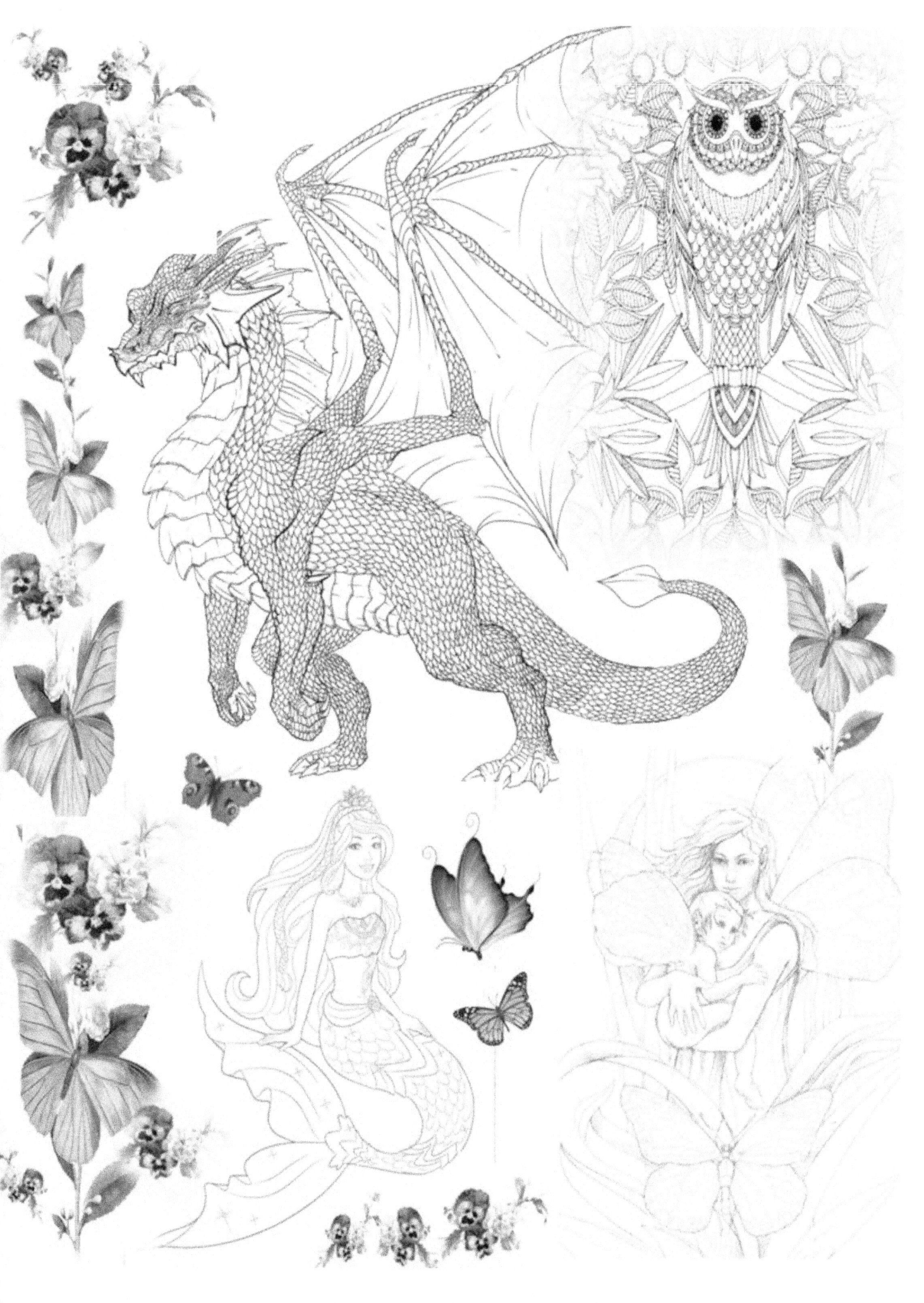

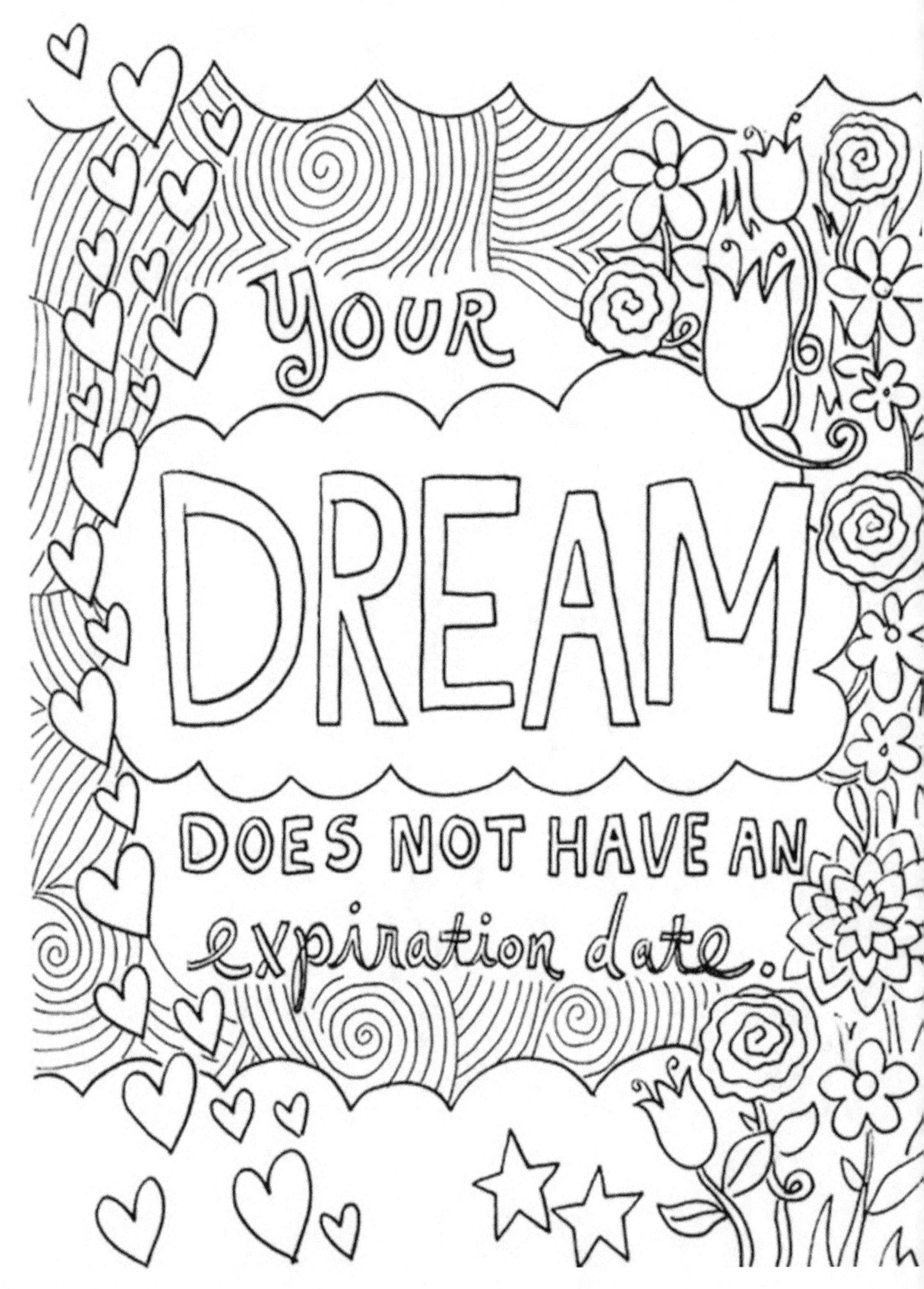

Your DREAM DOES NOT HAVE AN expiration date.

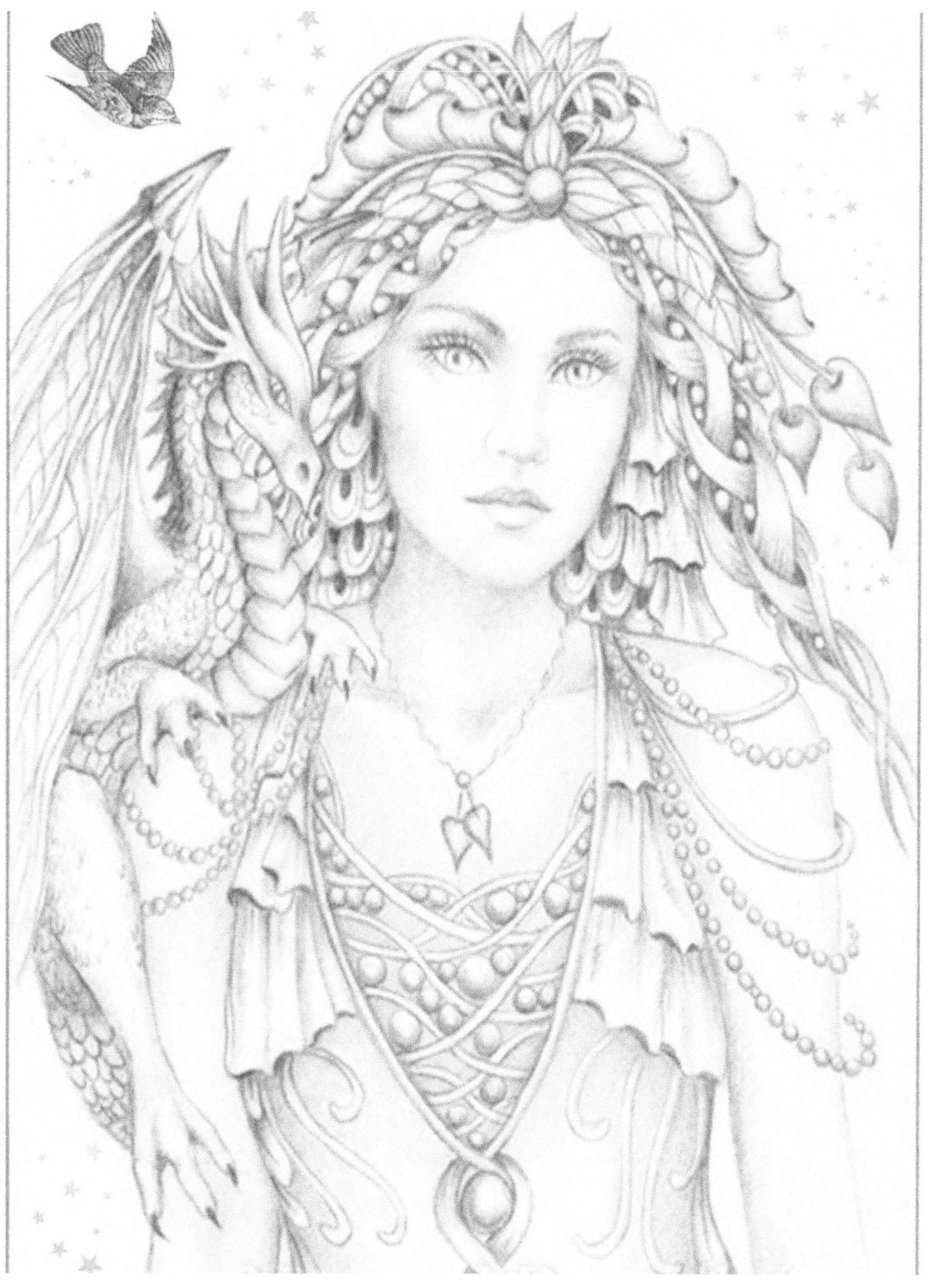

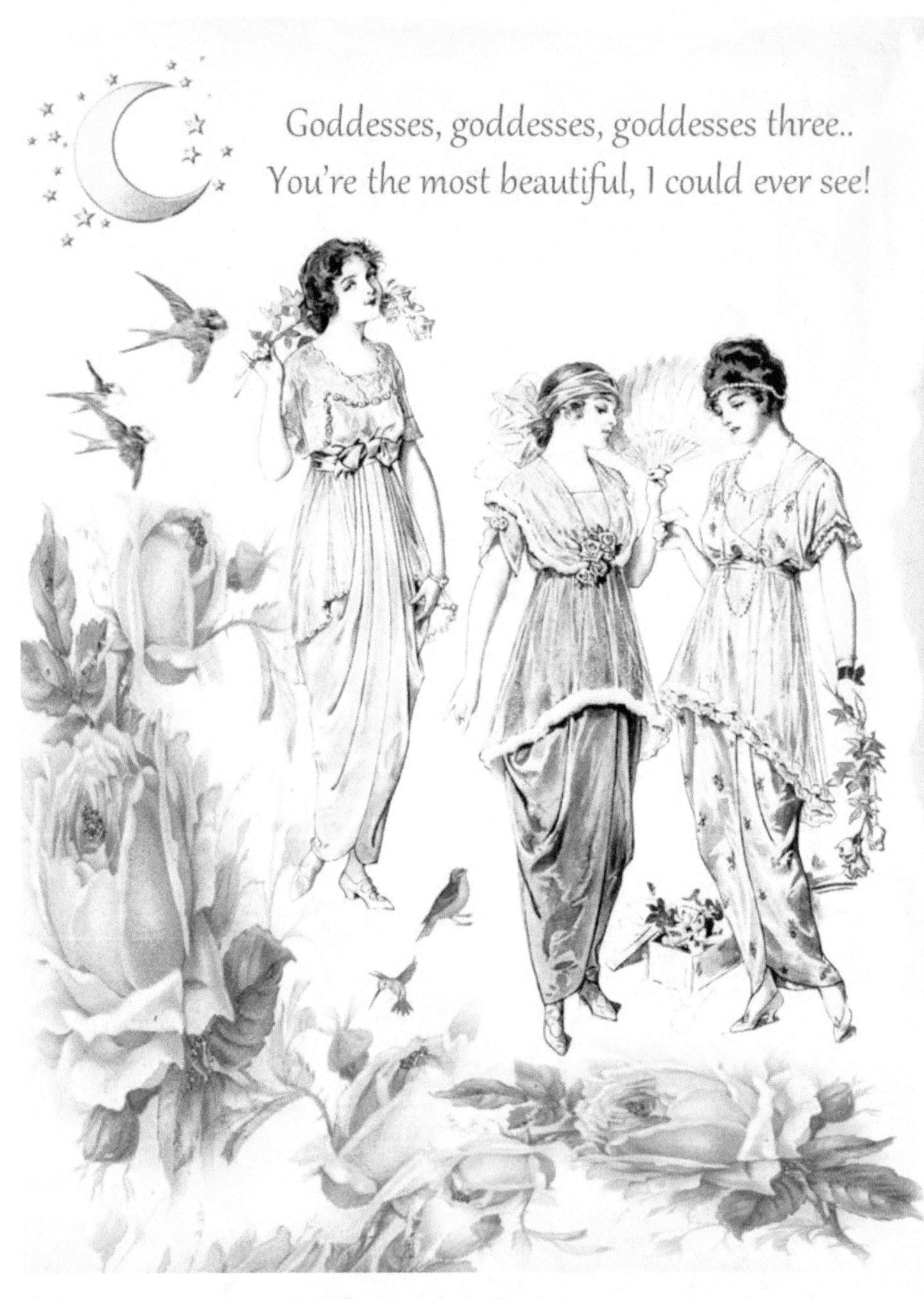

Goddesses, goddesses, goddesses three..
You're the most beautiful, I could ever see!

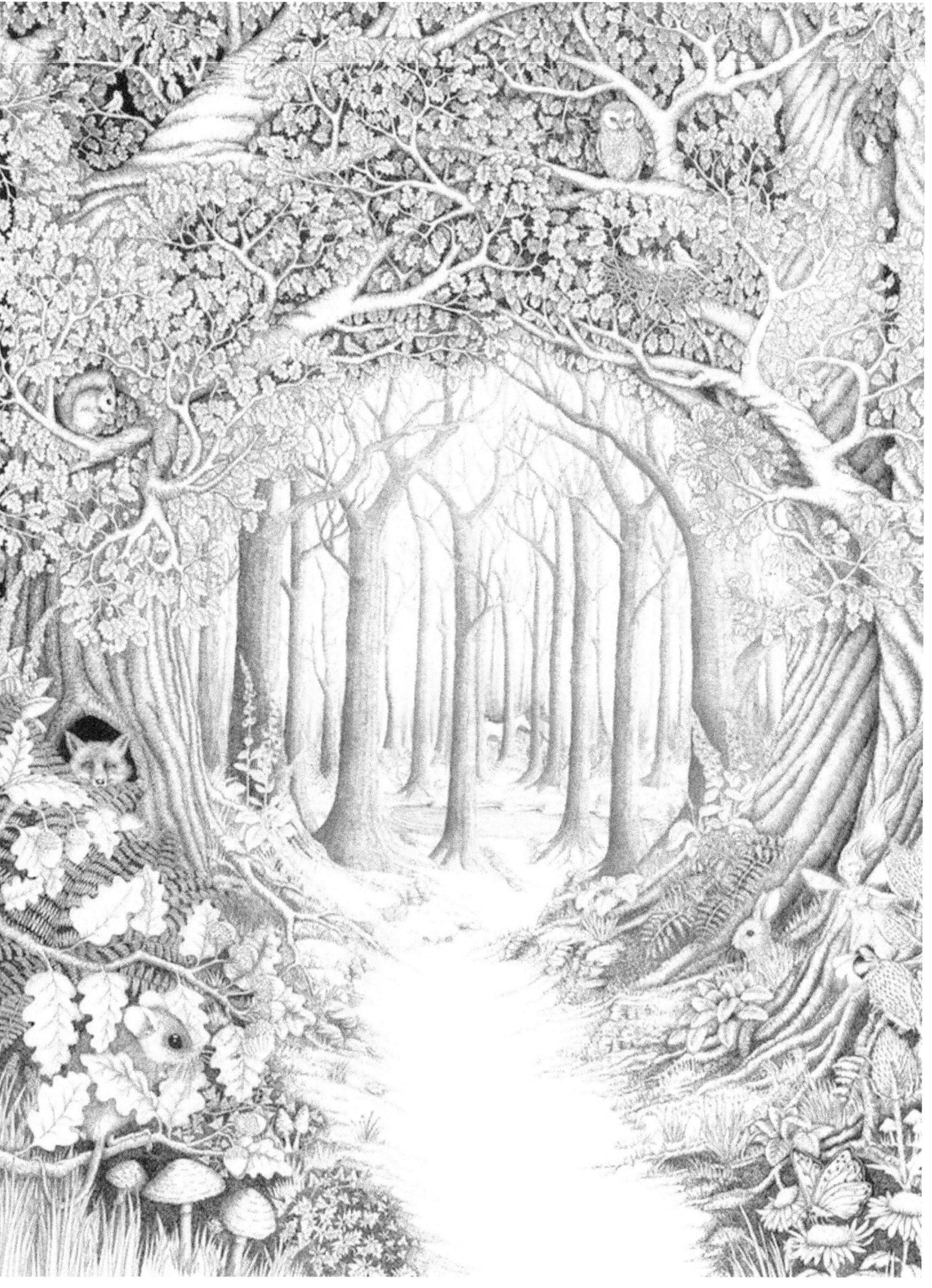

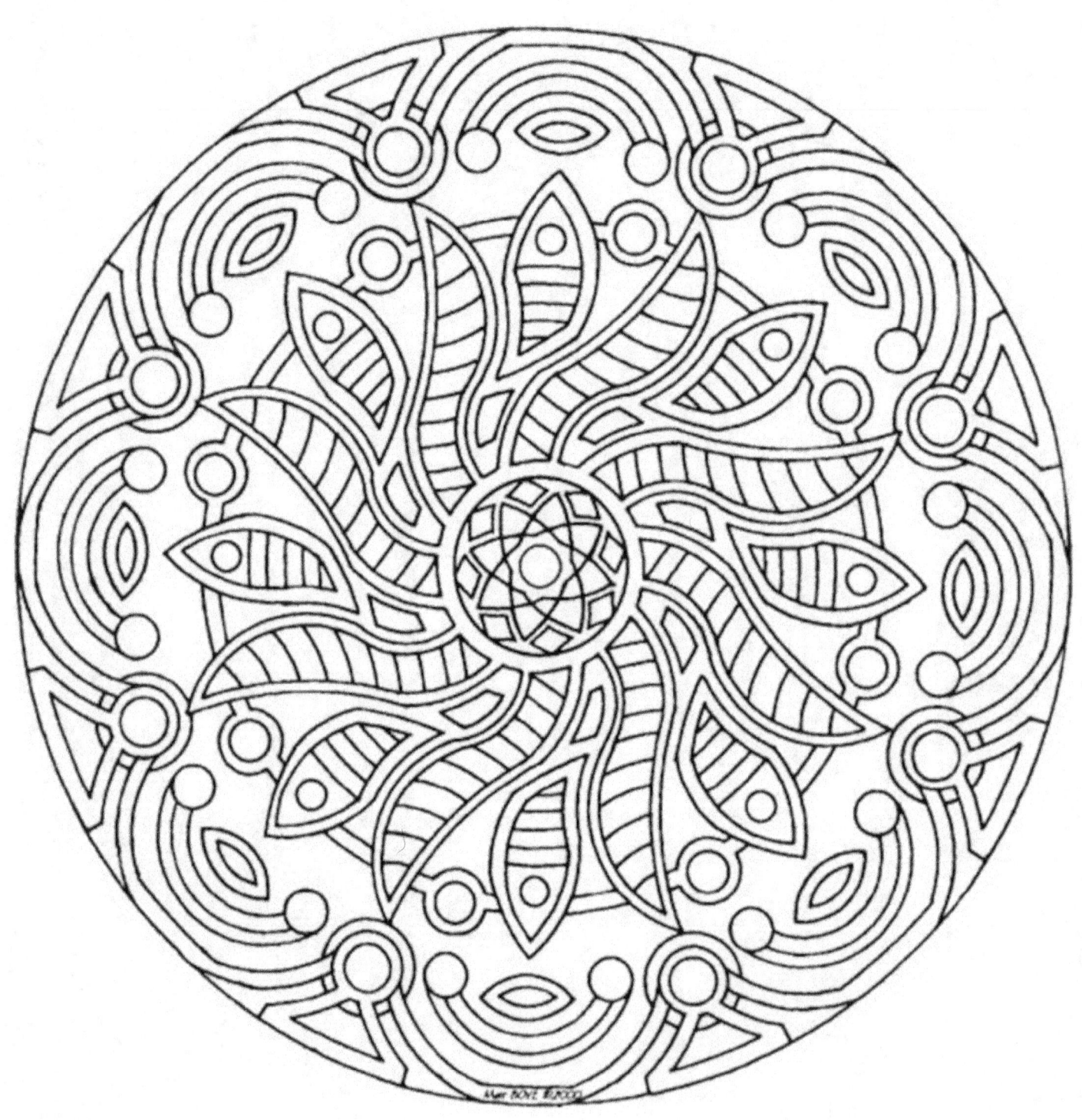

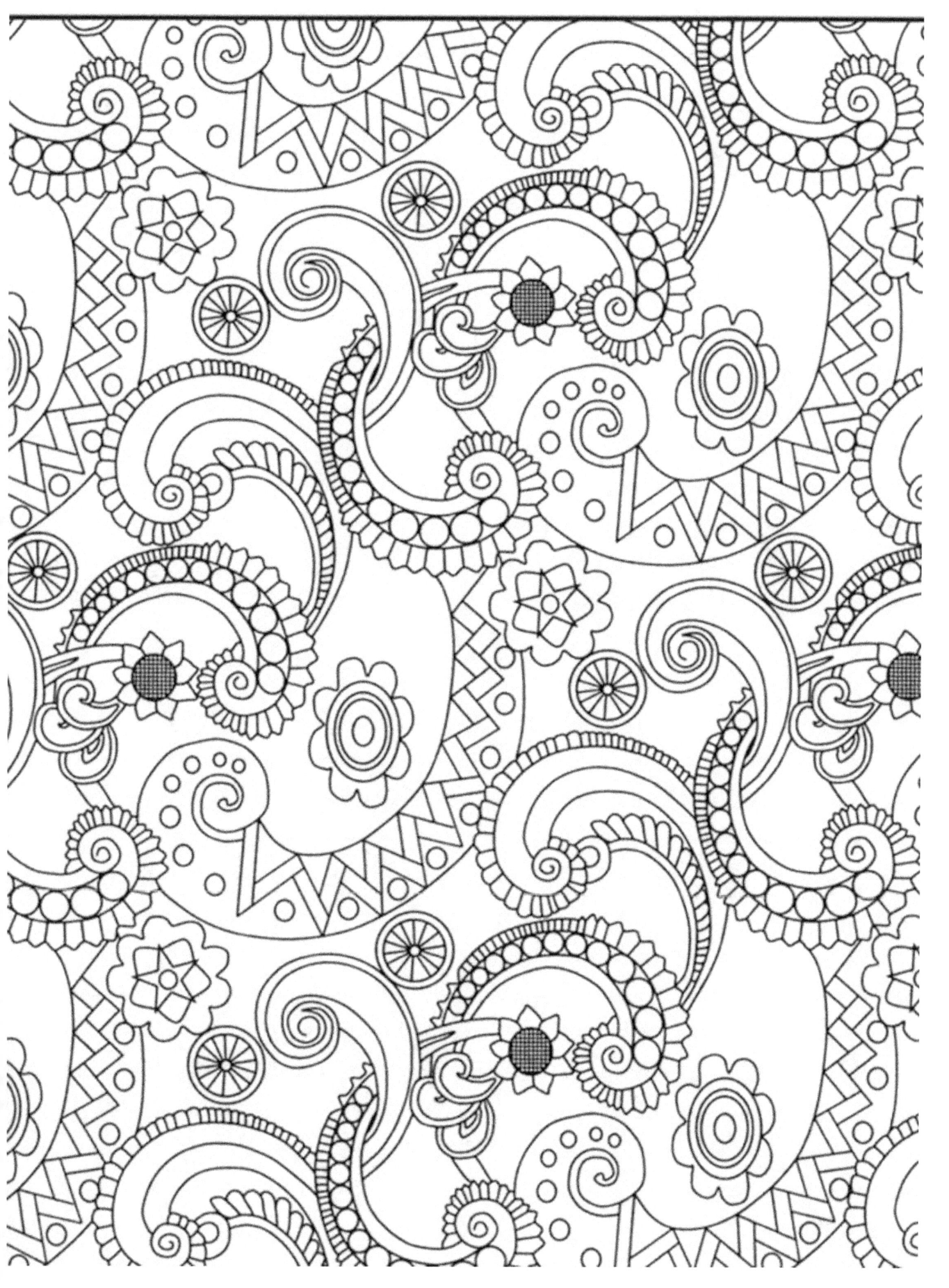

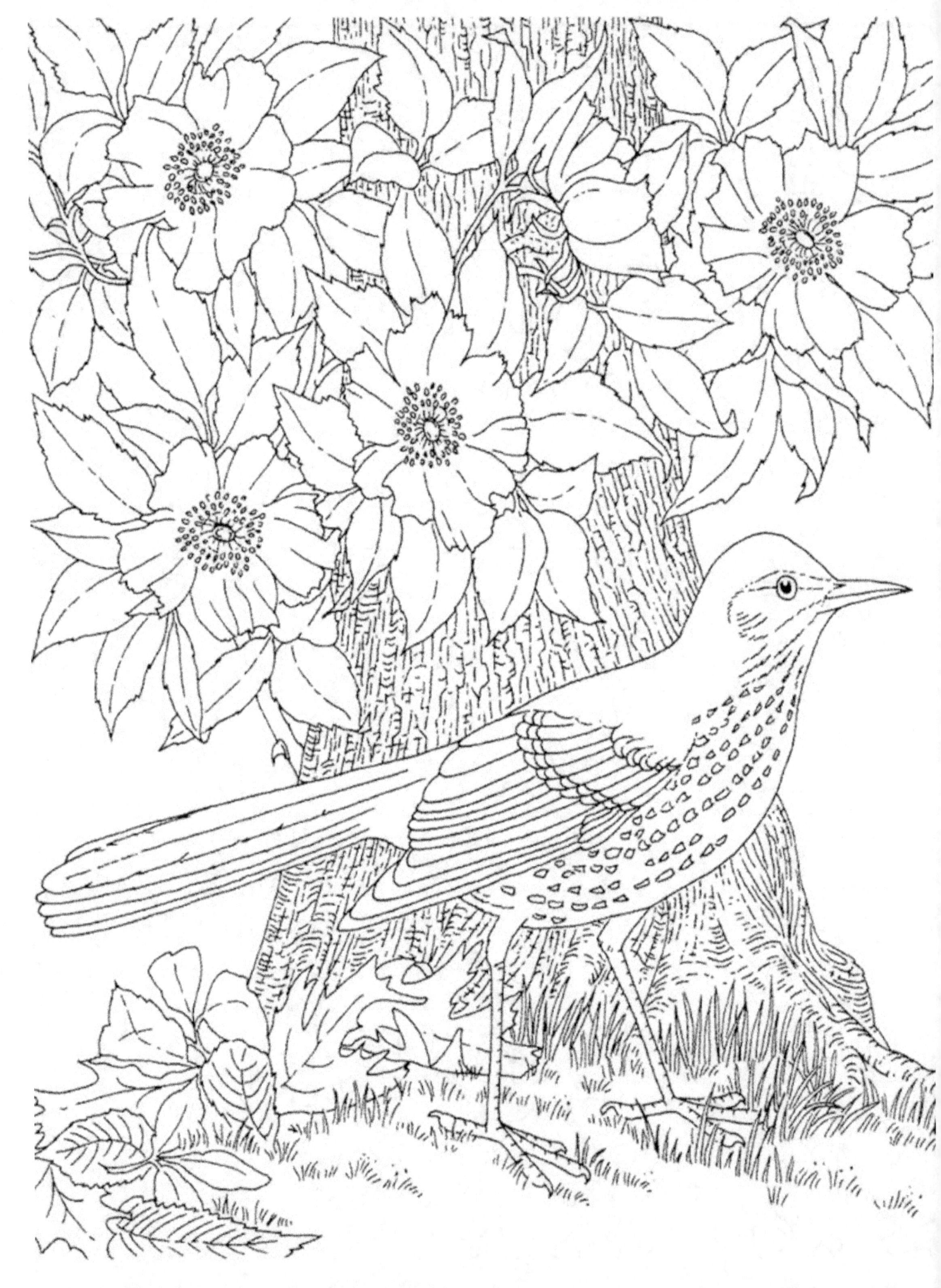

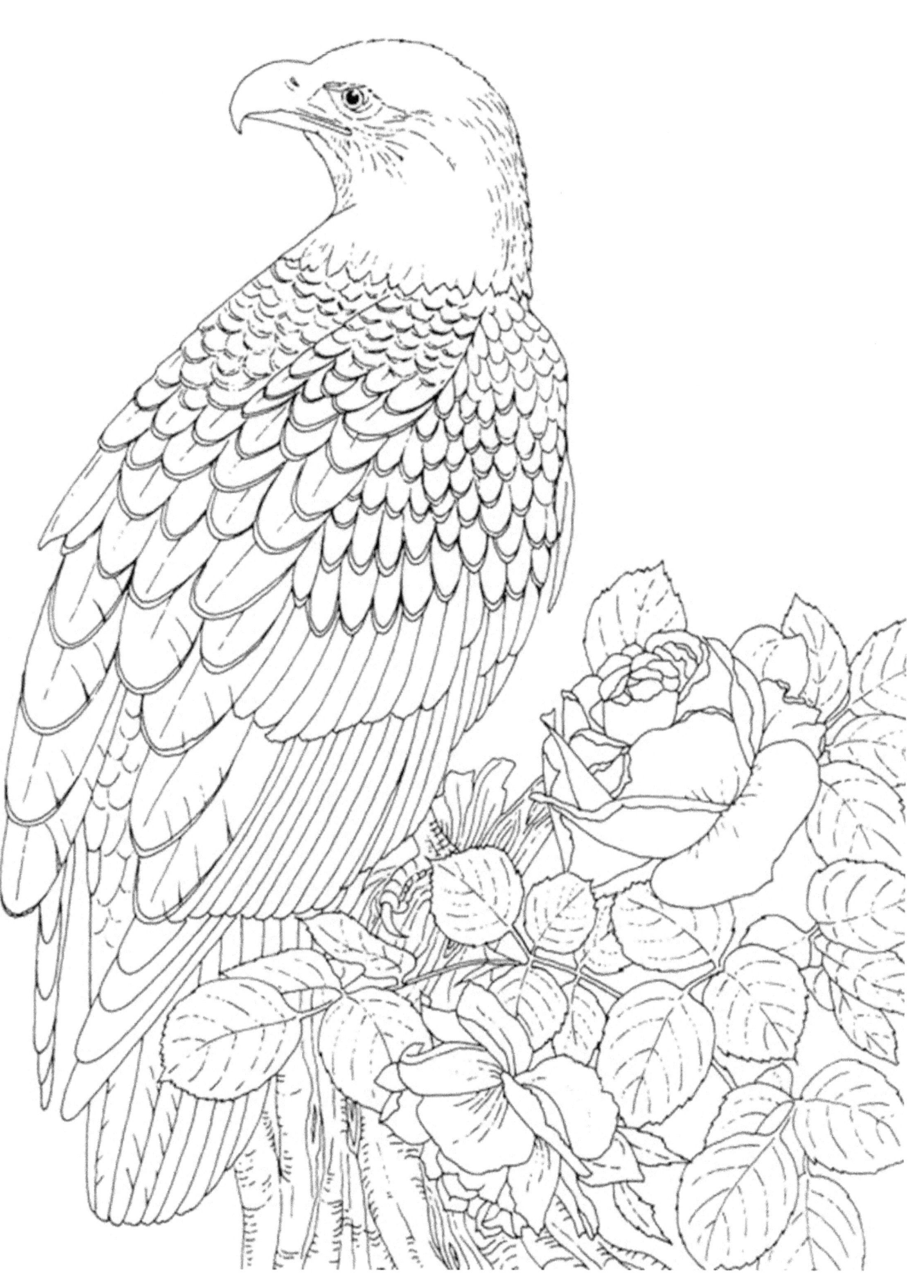

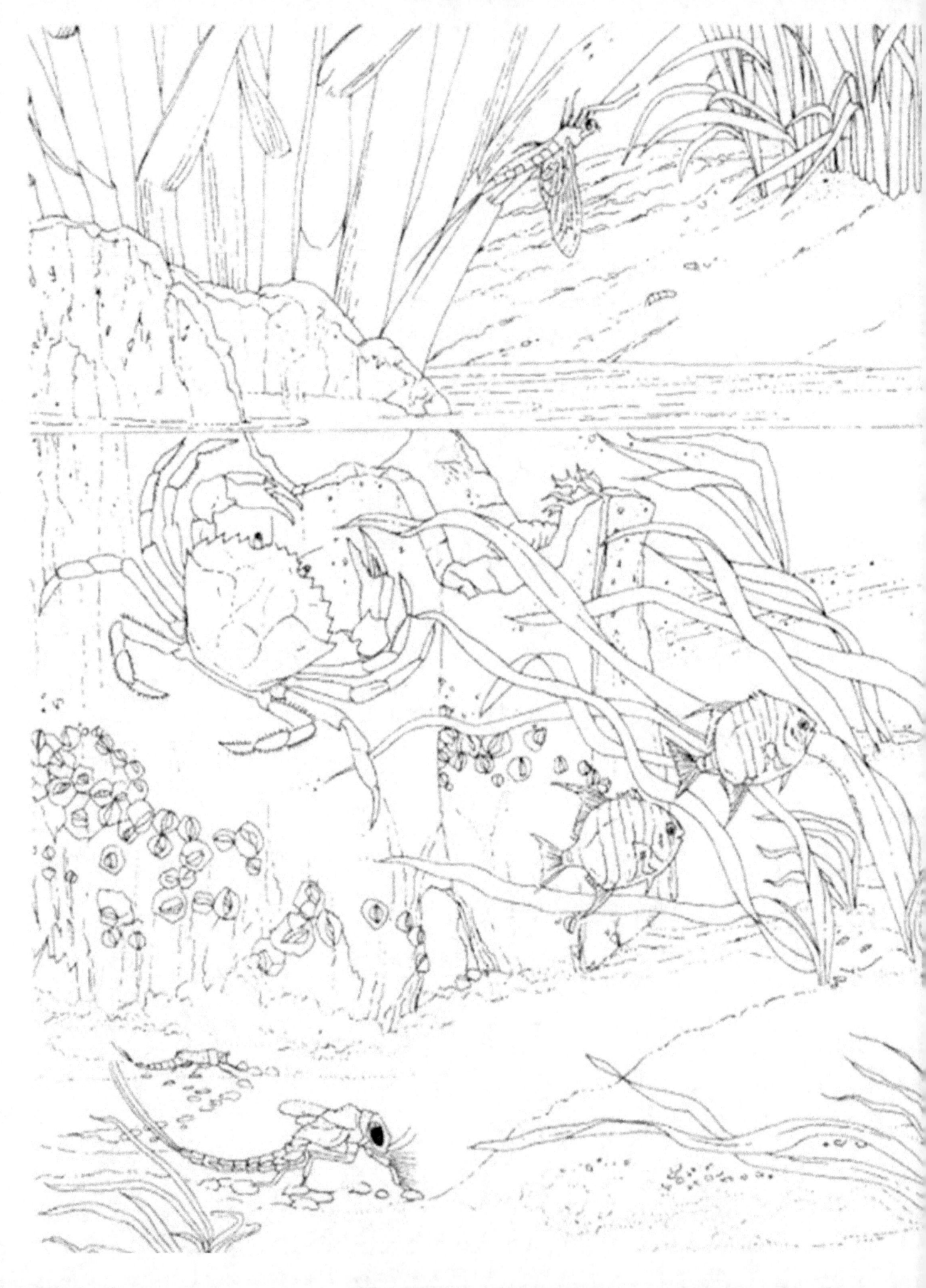

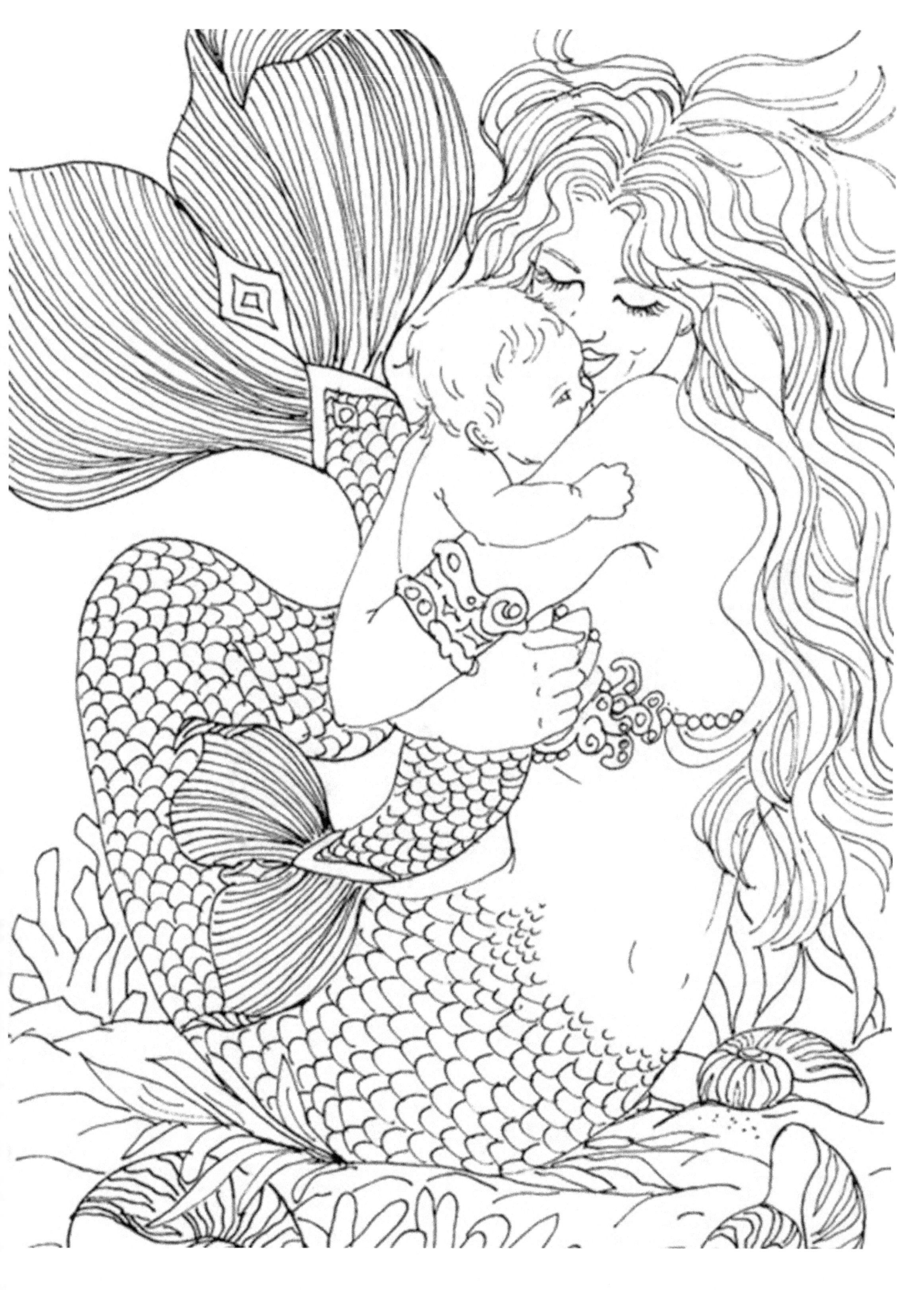

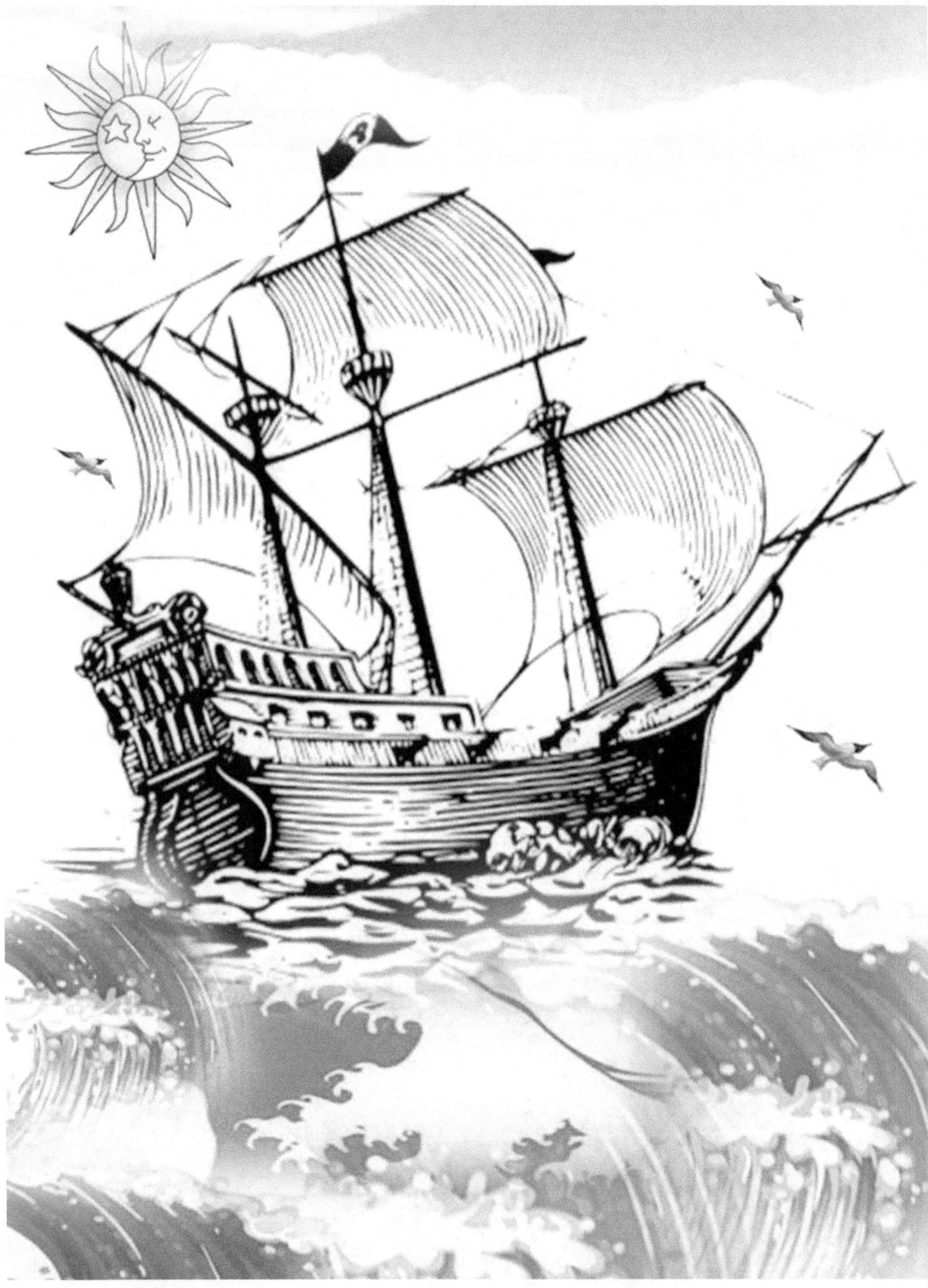

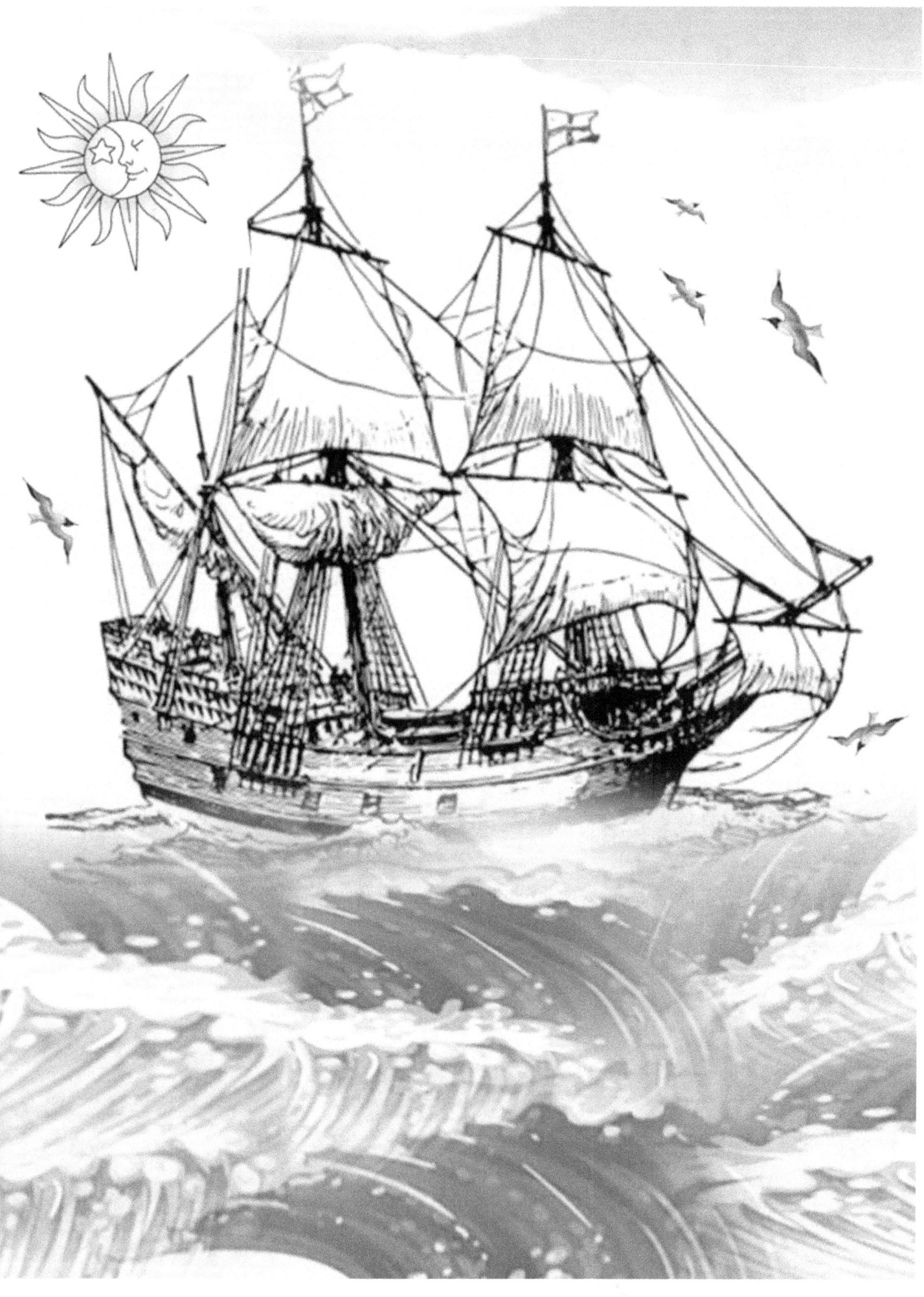

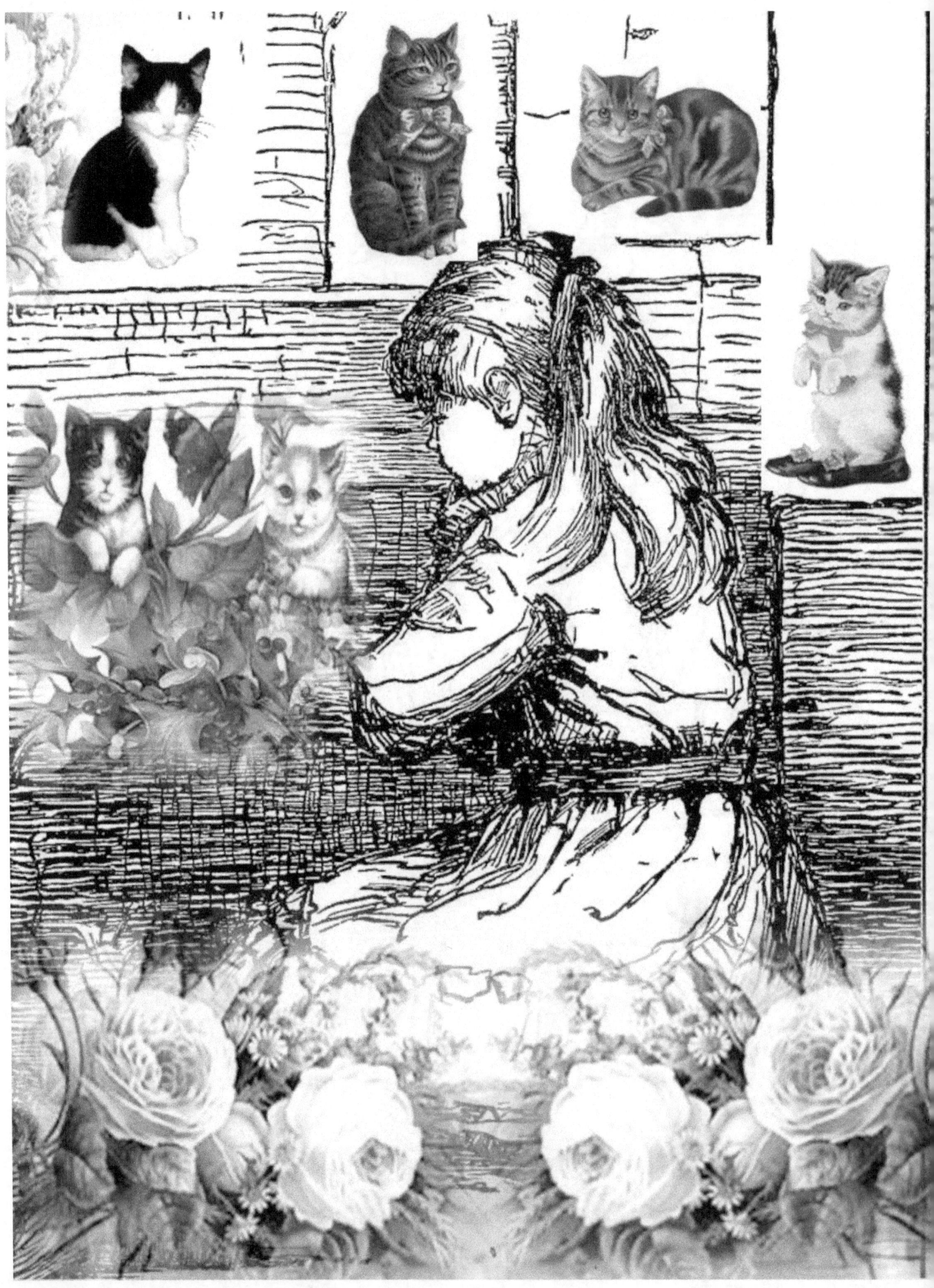

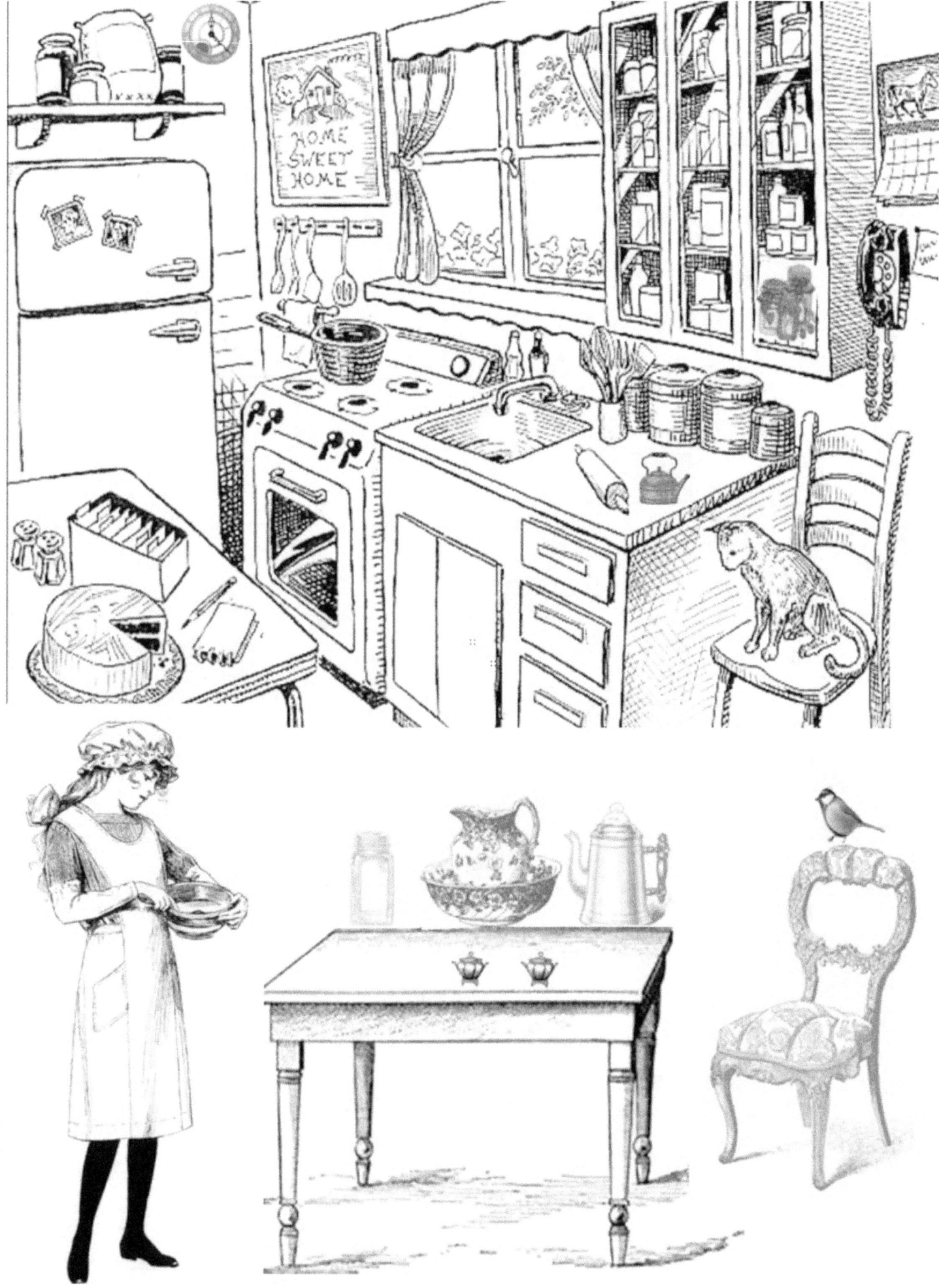

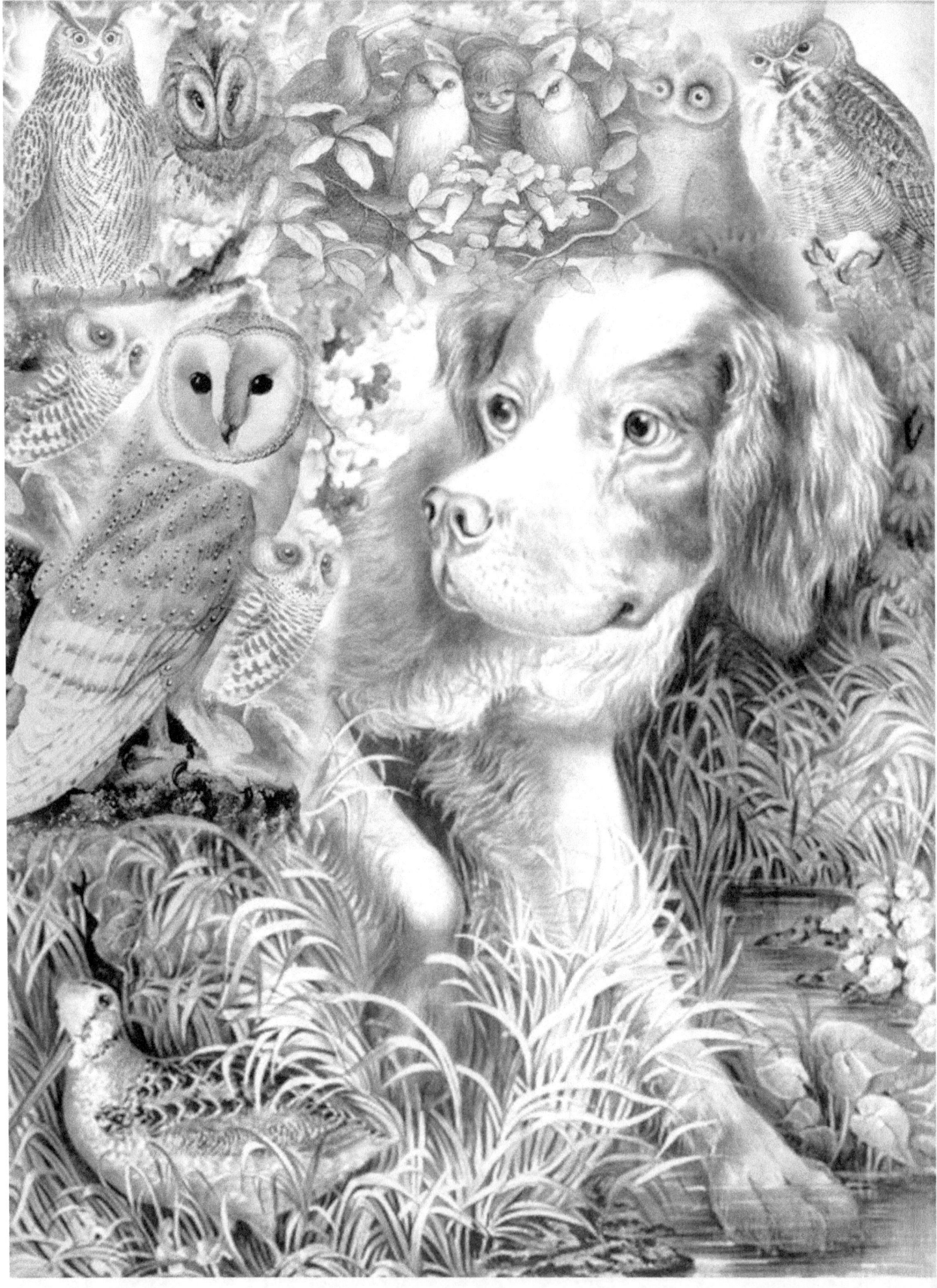

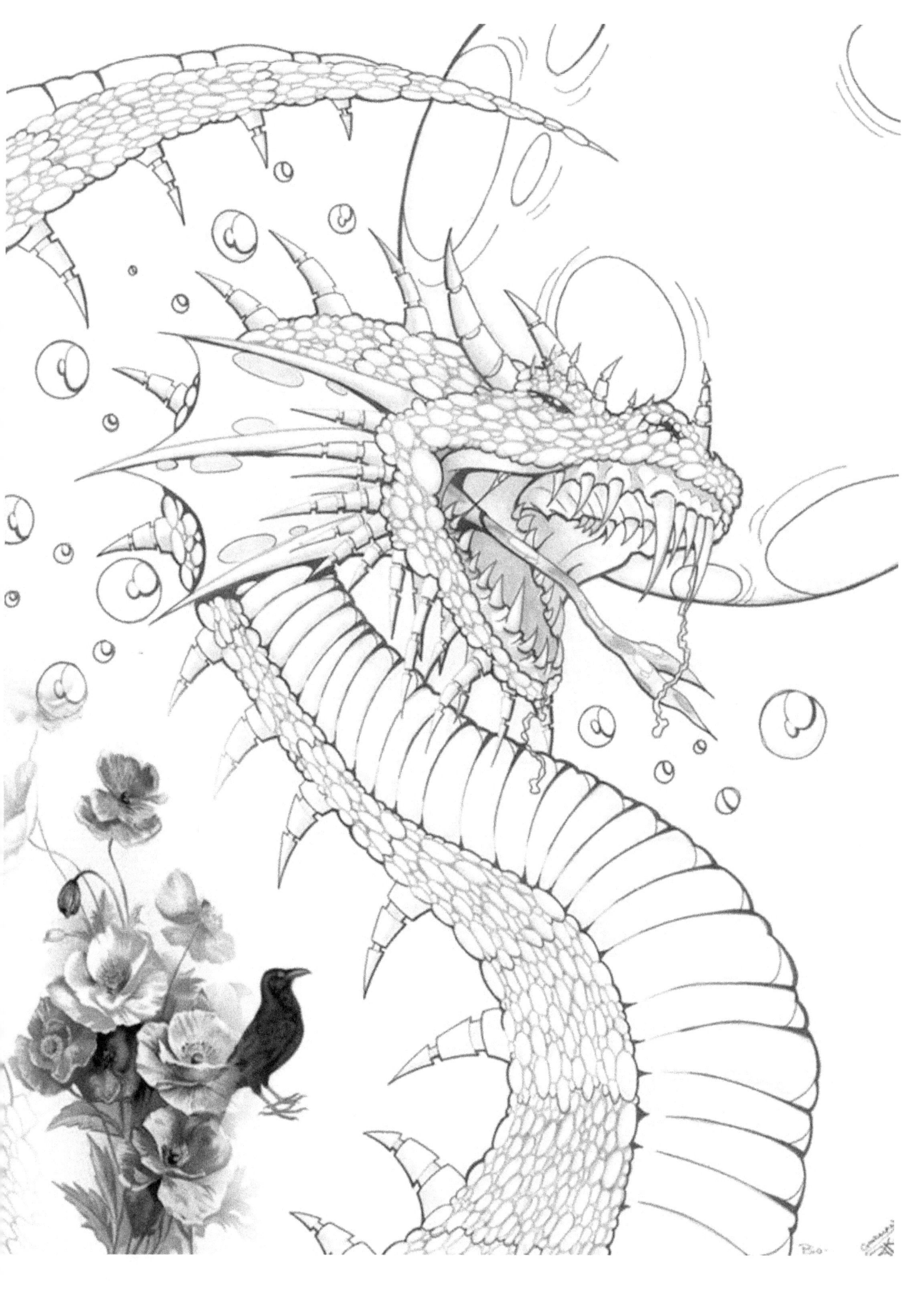

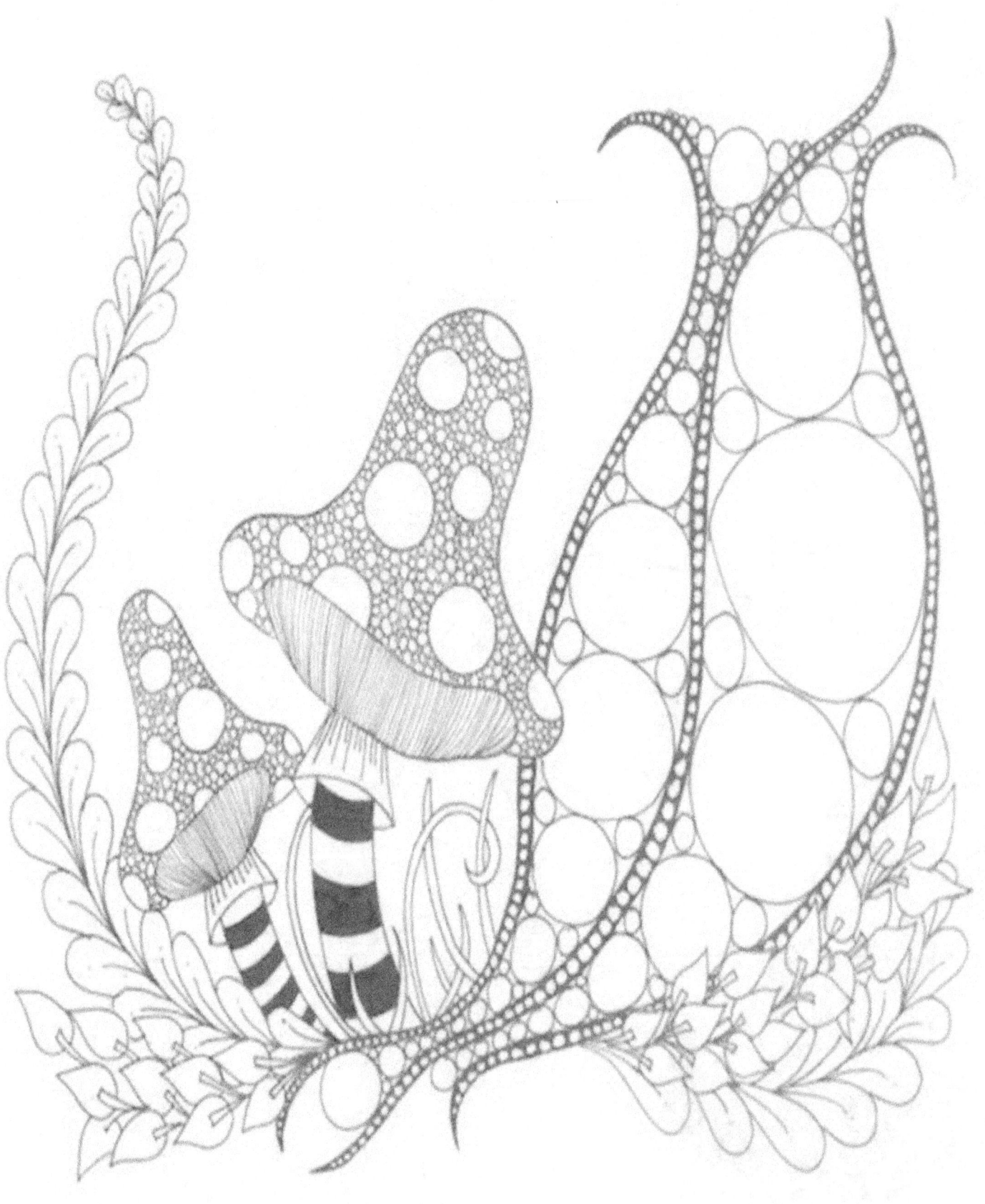

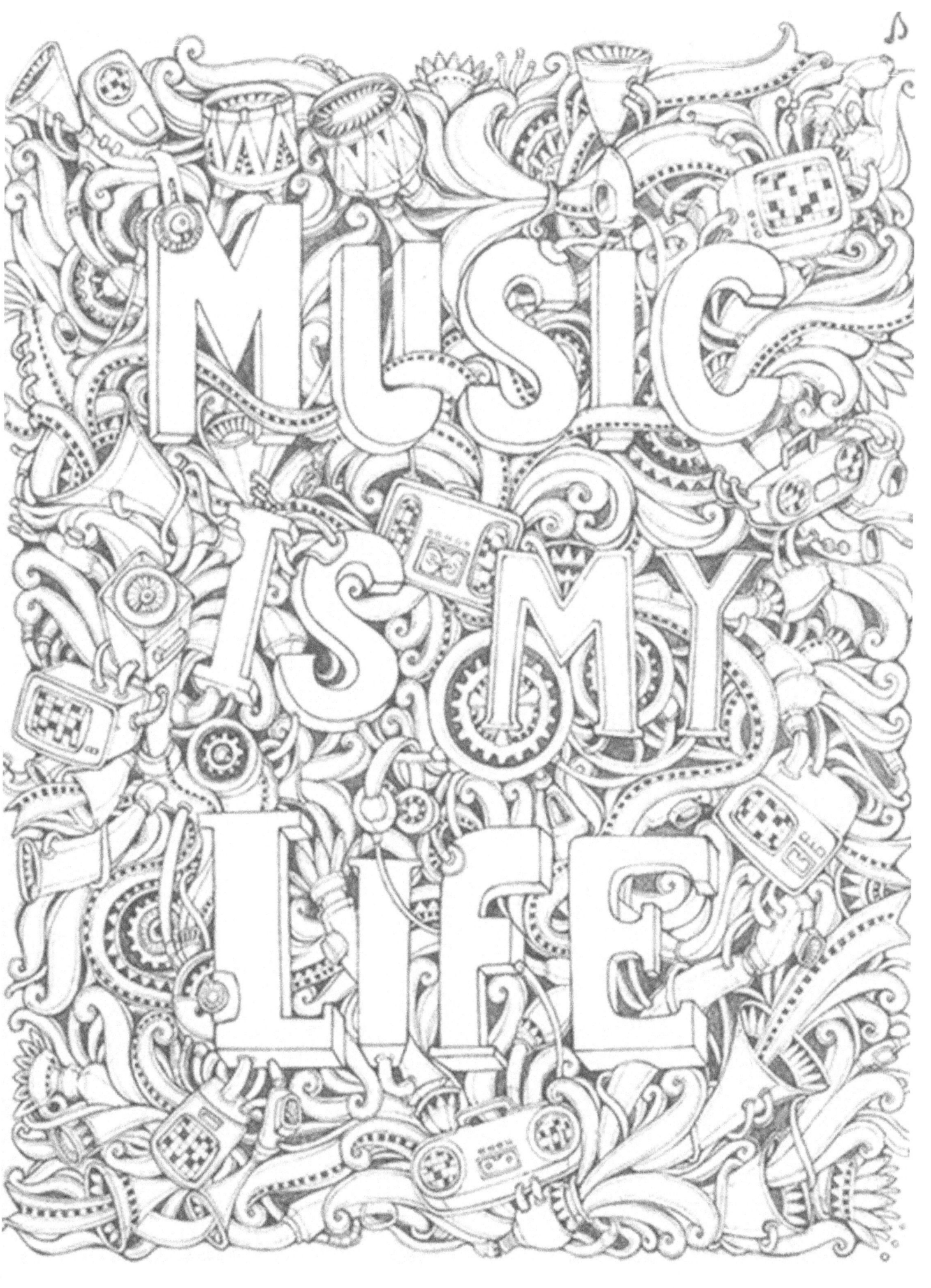

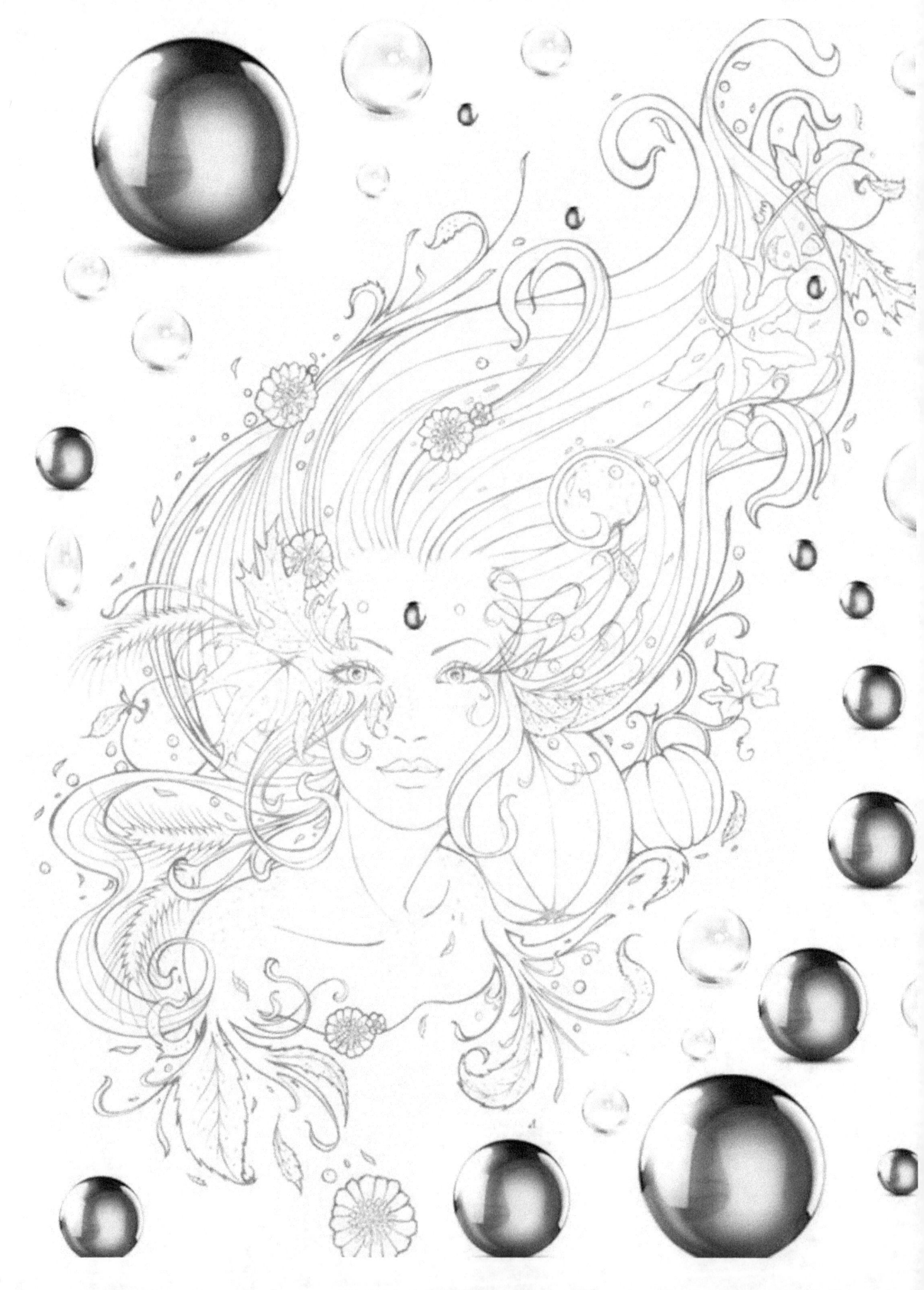

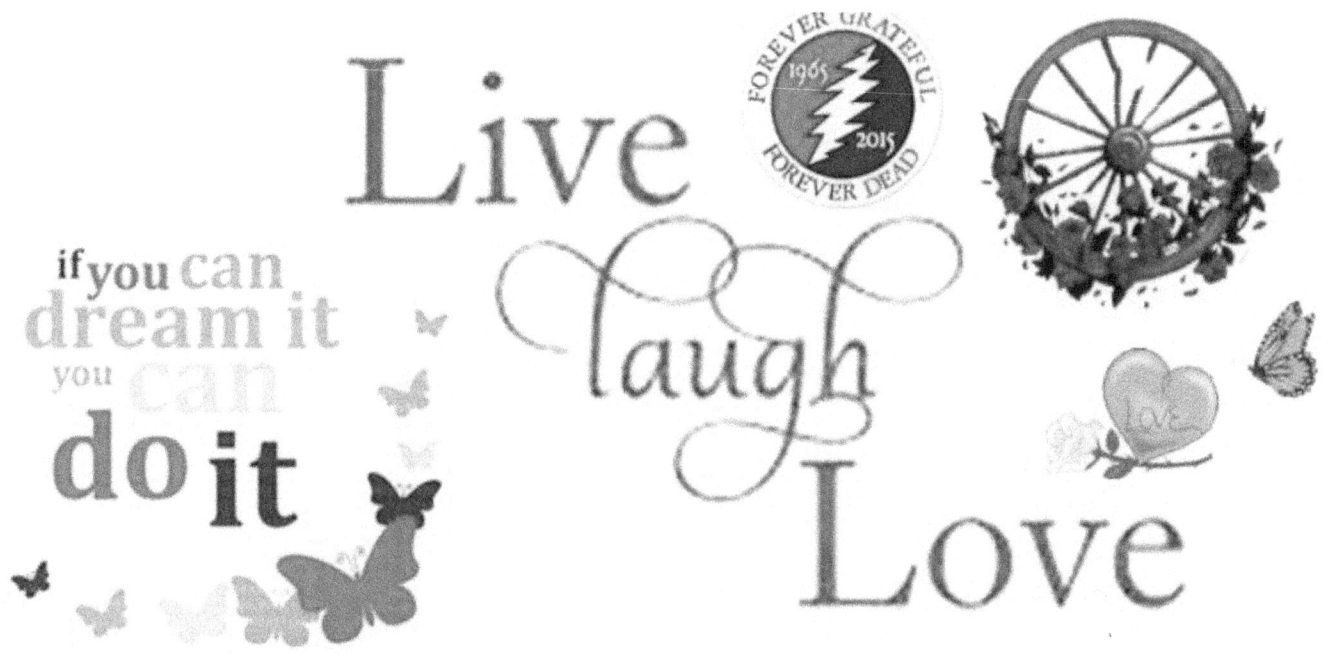

Live Laugh Love

if you can dream it you can do it

This book is dedicated to my good friend... ♥ Debbi

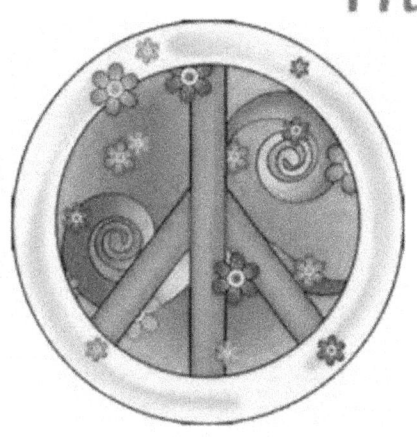

A s soon as I saw you,

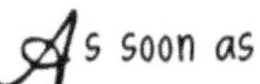

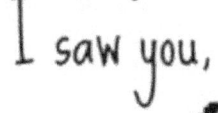

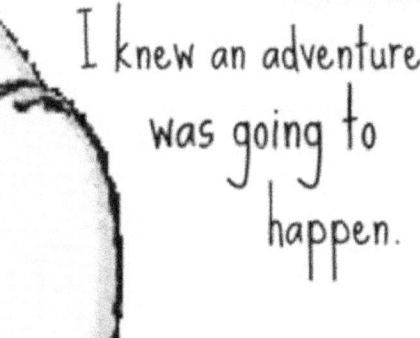

I knew an adventure was going to happen.

- Winnie the Pooh

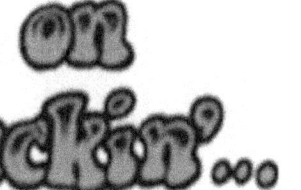

Keep on Truckin'...

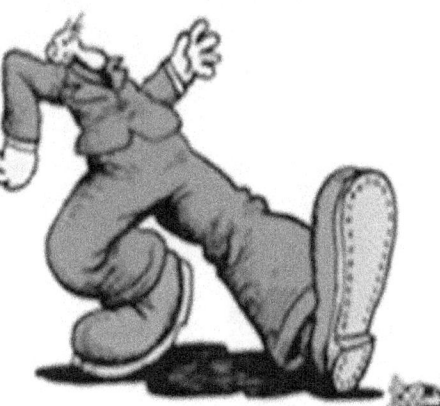

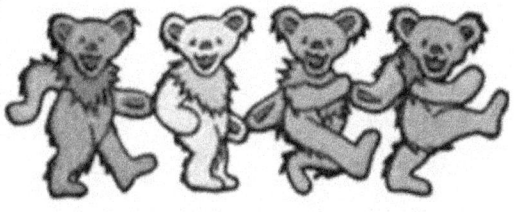

www.ingramcontent.com/pod-product-compliance
Lightning Source LLC
Chambersburg PA
CBHW080601190526
45169CB00007B/2842